Contents

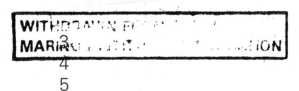

Licence

Text © Pat Hoodless

© 2003 Scholastic Ltd

Published by Scholastic Ltd, Villiers House,
Clarendon Avenue, Leamington Spa,
Warwickshire CV32 5PR

Printed by Bell & Bain Ltd, Glasgow

5 6 7 8 9 0   7 8 9 0 1 2

British Library Cataloguing-in-Publication Data
A catalogue record for this book is available from
the British Library.

ISBN 0-439-98451-3
ISBN 978-0439-98451-5

Visit our website at
www.scholastic.co.uk

CD developed in association with
Footmark Media Ltd

Author
Pat Hoodless

Editor
Dulcie Booth

Assistant Editor
Gaynor Spry

Series Designer
Joy Monkhouse

Designer
Clare Brewer

Cover photographs
© Photodisc
© Stockbyte

Acknowledgements

Extracts from the National Curriculum for England © Crown copyright material is reproduced
with the permission of the Controller of HMSO and the Queen's Printer for Scotland.

Every effort has been made to trace copyright holders and the publishers apologise for any
omissions.

Made with Macromedia is a
trademark of Macromedia, Inc.
Director ®
Copyright © 1984-2000
Macromedia, Inc.

Minimum Specifications:
PC: Windows 98 SE or higher
Processor: Pentium 2 (or equivalent) 400
MHz
RAM: 128 Mb
CD-ROM drive: 48x (52x preferred)

MAC: OS 9.2 (OSX preferred)
Processor: G3 400 MHz
RAM: 128Mb
CD-ROM drive: 48x (52x preferred)

List of resources on the CD-ROM

The page numbers refer to the teacher's notes provided in this book.

INTRODUCTION

This book and CD support the teaching and learning based on the QCA Scheme of Work for history at Key Stage Two. The CD provides a large bank of visual (and oral) resources. The book provides teacher's notes, background information, ideas for discussion and activities to accompany the CD resources, along with photocopiable pages to support the teaching. The resources have been selected to meet the requirements for resources outlined in the QCA units 'Why did Henry VIII marry six times?' and 'What were the differences between the lives of rich and poor people in Tudor times?'. They also cover the topics of Wallace and Bruce, of relevance to the history curriculum for Scotland. Additional resources and ideas have also been included, however, to enable teachers to develop and broaden these areas of study if they wish.

The resources and activities are not intended to be used rigidly, however, since they do not provide a structure for teaching in themselves. The teacher's notes provide ideas for discussion and activities which focus on the 'Knowledge, skills and understanding' of the National Curriculum for history. They aim to guide teachers in developing the children's skills and teaching concepts fundamental to an understanding of what it is to learn about the past. Detailed units of work and lesson plans will need to be developed alongside the ideas presented here, based, to a greater or lesser degree, on the QCA Schemes of Work and the History Curriculum for Scotland. The Schemes and Curriculum, however, will be more appropriate and relevant to your particular class, if you adapt them to suit your own needs and requirements.

In this book, there is an emphasis on developing children's awareness and understanding of chronology, of asking and answering questions, and of investigating historical sources and communicating findings in a variety of ways. Above all, the activities and discussions aim to build clear links between the firsthand experience they gain from using the resources on the CD and their developing awareness of the past.

Links with other subjects
Literacy
There are a number of close links between the topics covered in this book and literacy. The discussion activities contribute directly to the requirements for speaking and listening, as do the drama and role-play activities. The stories and accounts may be used in shared reading during the Literacy Hour, or to provide a stimulus for shared, guided or independent writing. There is considerable opportunity for the children to develop their independent writing skills in the form of diary entries and letters. Pictures from the CD can be printed to stimulate independent reading, writing and research, or to illustrate it. They may also be used to illustrate the timelines or sequence lines created in the course of each topic.

Art and design
There are similarly close links with art and design. Much work at Key Stage 2 needs to be visual. Wherever possible, activities in the teacher's notes make extensive use of drawing to extend the children's understanding of a particular topic or concept. For example, in drawing detailed pictures of Tudor artefacts they will develop their observational skills and improve their accuracy and precision in their artwork. Working with portraits will also develop their skills in source analysis through the use of art.

ICT
Finally, there are clear links with information technology. ICT is constantly useful throughout, particularly in terms of providing an inexhaustible resource for children to use in carrying out research into specific aspects of each topic.

HOW TO USE THE CD-ROM

Windows NT users
If you use Windows NT you may see the following error message: 'The procedure entry point Process32First could not be located in the dynamic link library KERNEL32.dll'. Click on **OK** and the CD will autorun with no further problems.

Setting up your computer for optimal use
On opening, the CD will alert you if changes are needed in order to operate the CD at its optimal use. There are three changes you may be advised to make:

Viewing resources at their maximum screen size
To see images at their maximum screen size, your screen display needs to be set to 800 x 600 pixels. In order to adjust your screen size you will need to **Quit** the program.

If using a PC, open the **Control Panel**. Select **Display** and then **Settings**. Adjust the **Desktop Area** to 800 x 600 pixels. Click on **OK** and then restart the program.

If using a Mac, from the **Apple** menu select **Control Panels** and then **Monitors** to adjust the screen size.

Adobe Acrobat Reader
To print high-quality versions of images and to view and print the photocopiable pages on the CD you need **Adobe Acrobat Reader** installed on your computer. If you do not have it installed already, a version is provided on the CD. To install this version **Quit** the 'Ready Resources' program.

If using a PC, right-click on the **Start** menu on your desktop and choose **Explore**. Click on the + sign to the left of the CD drive entitled 'Ready Resources' and open the folder called 'Acrobat Reader Installer'. Run the program contained in this folder to install **Adobe Acrobat Reader**.

If using a Mac, double click on the 'Ready Resources' icon on the desktop and on the 'Acrobat Reader Installer' folder. Run the program contained in this folder to install **Adobe Acrobat Reader**.

PLEASE NOTE: If you do not have **Adobe Acrobat Reader** installed, you will not be able to print high-quality versions of images, or to view or print photocopiable pages (although these are provided in the accompanying book and can be photocopied).

QuickTime
In order to view the videos and listen to the audio on this CD you will need to have **QuickTime version 5 or later** installed on your computer. If you do not have it installed already or have an older version of QuickTime, the latest version can be downloaded at http://www.apple.com/quicktime/download/win.html. If you choose to install this version, **Quit** the 'Ready Resources' program.

PLEASE NOTE: If you do not have **QuickTime** installed you will be unable to view the films.

Menu screen
▶ Click on the **Resource Gallery** of your choice to view the resources available under that topic.
▶ Click on **Complete Resource Gallery** to view all the resources available on the CD.
▶ Click on **Photocopiable Resources (PDF format)** to view a list of the photocopiables provided in the book that accompanies this CD.
▶ **Back**: click to return to the **opening screen**. Click **Continue** to move to the **Menu screen**.
▶ **Quit**: click **Quit** to close the menu program and progress to the **Quit screen.** If you quit from the **Quit screen** you will exit the CD. If you do not quit you will return to the **Menu screen**.

Resource Galleries
▶ **Help**: click **Help** to find support on accessing and using images.
▶ **Back to menu**: click here to return to the **Menu screen**.
▶ **Quit**: click here to move to the **Quit screen** – see **Quit** above.

Viewing images

Small versions of each image are shown in the Resource Gallery. Click and drag the slider on the slide bar to scroll through the images in the Resource Gallery, or click on the arrows to move the images frame by frame. Roll the pointer over an image to see the caption.

▶ Click on an image to view the screen-sized version of it.

▶ To return to the Resource Gallery click on **Back to Resource Gallery**.

Viewing videos

Click on the video icon of your choice in the Resource Gallery. In order to view the videos on this CD, you will need to have **QuickTime** installed on your computer (see 'Setting up your computer for optimal use' above).

Once at the video screen, use the buttons on the bottom of the video screen to operate the video. The slide bar can be used for a fast forward and rewind. To return to the Resource Gallery click on **Back to Resource Gallery**.

Listening to sound recordings

Click on the required sound icon. Use the buttons or the slide bar to hear the sound. A transcript will be displayed on the viewing screen where appropriate. To return to the Resource Gallery, click on **Back to Resource Gallery**.

Printing

Click on the image to view it (see 'Viewing images' above). There are two print options:

Print using Acrobat enables you to print a high-quality version of an image. Choosing this option means that the image will open as a read-only page in **Adobe Acrobat** and in order to access these files you will need to have already installed **Adobe Acrobat Reader** on your computer (see 'Setting up your computer for optimal use' above). To print the selected resource, select **File** and then **Print**. Once you have printed the resource **minimise** or **close** the Adobe screen using — or **X** in the top right-hand corner of the screen. Return to the Resource Gallery by clicking on **Back to Resource Gallery**.

Simple print enables you to print a lower quality version of the image without the need to use **Adobe Acrobat Reader**. Select the image and click on the **Simple print** option. After printing, click on **Back to Resource Gallery**.

Slideshow presentation

If you would like to present a number of resources without having to return to the Resource Gallery and select a new image each time, you can compile a slideshow. Click on the **+** tabs at the top of each image in the Resource Gallery you would like to include in your presentation (pictures, sound and video can be included). It is important that you click on the images in the order in which you would like to view them (a number will appear on each tab to confirm the order). If you would like to change the order, click on **Clear slideshow** and begin again. Once you have selected your images – up to a maximum of 20 – click on **Play slideshow** and you will be presented with the first of your selected resources. To move to the next selection in your slideshow click on **Next slide**, to see a previous resource click on **Previous slide**. You can end your slideshow presentation at any time by clicking on **Resource Gallery**. Your slideshow selection will remain selected until you **Clear slideshow** or return to the **Menu screen**.

Viewing on an interactive whiteboard or data projector

Resources can be viewed directly from the CD. To make viewing easier for a whole class, use a large monitor, data projector or interactive whiteboard. For group, paired or individual work, the resources can be viewed from the computer screen.

Photocopiable resources (PDF format)

To view or print a photocopiable resource page, click on the required title in the list and the page will open as a read-only page in **Adobe Acrobat**. In order to access these files you will need to have already installed **Adobe Acrobat Reader** on your computer (see 'Setting up your computer for optimal use' above). To print the selected resource select **File** and then **Print**. Once you have printed the resource **minimise** or **close** the Adobe screen using — or **X** in the top right-hand corner of the screen. This will take you back to the list of PDF files. To return to the **Menu screen**, click on **Back**.

HENRY VIII

Content, skills and concepts

This chapter on Henry VIII relates to Unit 7 in the QCA Scheme of Work for history at Key Stage 2. Together with the Henry VIII Resource Gallery on the CD it introduces a range of visual and written resources that focus partly on the question, 'Why did Henry VIII marry six times?', and also on other aspects of the Tudor period. These can be used in teaching about the Tudor monarchy and the personalities of key characters, important events, everyday life, as well as some of the discoveries of Tudor artefacts found on the *Mary Rose*. It also provides materials to support the teaching of key historical concepts relevant to this period and theme.

Children will already have gained experience, while working on other history units, of sequencing and using timelines, the use of time-related vocabulary, asking and answering questions, and using pictures and written sources. Recounting stories about the past, and looking for similarities and differences between the past and the present are all other prior learning activities which will have introduced relevant skills and concepts to the children in previous years, before they progress to the skills and concepts in this unit. Suggestions for the further development of these skills form part of this chapter.

Resources on the CD-ROM

A map showing Europe in Tudor times, portraits of the key royal characters and Henry's wives, along with photographs of artefacts recovered from the *Mary Rose* are provided on the CD. An audio recording of 'Greensleeves' (at one time thought to have been composed by Henry VIII) played on traditional Tudor instruments is also provided. Teacher's notes containing background information and ideas for further work on them are included in this chapter.

Photocopiable pages

Photocopiable resources within the book (and also provided in PDF format on the CD) include:
▶ timelines
▶ word and sentence cards which highlight the essential vocabulary of this topic
▶ a story about Anne of Cleves
▶ a firsthand account about Henry VIII.

The teacher's notes that accompany the photocopiable pages include suggestions for developing discussion and using them as whole class, group or individual activities. The account and story have been written at different reading levels and introduce topic-specific vocabulary. The story about Anne of Cleves aims to interest the children in the marriage alliances whilst the firsthand account of Henry illustrates a contemporary view and shows children how the Tudors wrote.

History skills

Skills such as observing, describing, using time-related vocabulary, sequencing, using of a timeline, understanding the meaning of dates, comparing, inferring, listening, speaking, reading, writing and drawing are involved in the activities provided. For example, there is an opportunity to develop independent skills in sequencing through the use of the timeline of the main events of Henry's reign. The children can learn to use descriptive vocabulary to describe the different monarchs and wives and to describe the wide range of Tudor artefacts shown on the CD.

Historical understanding

In the course of the suggested tasks, a further overarching aim is for children to begin to develop a more detailed knowledge of the past and their ability to sequence and date events independently, through their understanding of the context and content of the factual information they use. They will begin to give reasons for events, use sources to find further information and be able to recount and rewrite the stories and accounts they have heard. They will also have the opportunity to extend their skills in using descriptive language and specific time-related terms in beginning to write their own factual accounts of the past.

NOTES ON THE CD-ROM RESOURCES

Young King Henry VIII

This portrait, painted by an unknown artist in about 1520, shows Henry VIII as a young man aged about 28. At this time he was still married to Catherine of Aragon but was becoming increasingly unhappy with the lack of a male heir – see also notes on Catherine of Aragon (page 9).

As a young man, Henry was much admired. He was tall, good looking and fair, an attribute which was considered most attractive at that time. In addition to this, Henry clearly possessed a wide range of social and intellectual skills which charmed those who met him. He was a keen sportsman and rider, regularly jousting and hunting. He was clever, a writer (he wrote a book condemning Lutheranism), a musician, a skilful dancer and a composer. (See the notes on Greensleeves, page 21). He enjoyed court life, especially the company of the young female courtiers, and is known to have had numerous affairs and relationships, one of which ultimately led to his divorce from Catherine of Aragon and his marriage to Anne Boleyn. It is likely that Henry fathered illegitimate children, one of whom we know was called Arthur.

Discussing the portrait
▶ Look carefully at the picture and ask the children what kind of picture they think this is, for example a painting; a portrait. Discuss the meaning of the word *portrait*.
▶ Ask if they know who it may be in the portrait. What type of person do they think it could be, for example famous, rich. Discuss why they think this is an important person, for example the clothes, hat, jewels.
▶ Explain that it is a portrait of Henry VIII as a young man. Discuss whether he appears young to the children, which he may not because of the beard.
▶ Notice the number of jewels he wears, for example the rings. Discuss what this may suggest about him, for example perhaps he was a little vain?
▶ Look closely at Henry's expression and discuss the words that could be used to describe his attitude, for example *piercing gaze*, *intense*, *hard*, *serious*.
▶ Discuss how portraits can sometimes tell us more about a person than just what they used to wear. Explain how we can sometimes see something of their personality in their pictures.

Activities
▶ Use the timeline of Henry's life (see photocopiable page 30) to place the date of this portrait. Look at how much longer he lived after it was painted. Suggest the children work out his age at the time of painting.
▶ Give the class the task of noting each item of Henry's dress, finding suitable words to describe them, for example *full sleeves*, *heavy chain*. Compare them with the pictures of 'Lady's bodice' and 'Man's tunic' (also provided on the CD – see Rich and poor in Tudor times Resource Gallery or Complete Resource Gallery).
▶ Give the children sets of word cards from photocopiable page 27 to describe Henry and ask them to select those which they think apply to this portrait.
▶ Challenge the children to ask their own questions about the portrait. Working in pairs, ask them to write answers to the questions devised by their partners.
▶ Provide a variety of art materials and set the children the task of creating their own picture of Henry as a young man.
▶ Compare this portrait with that of Henry in later years 'King Henry VIII when older' (provided on the CD and see also notes on this page and on page 9).
▶ Look at the portrait 'Catherine of Aragon' (provided on the CD and see also notes on page 9) to whom Henry was married at the time of this portrait.

King Henry VIII when older

This portrait of Henry VIII was painted by Hans Holbein, the court artist. Henry, at the age of about 48, is seen in an innovative standing pose, one which has come to characterise him throughout history. The portrait is detailed and provides considerable evidence of Henry's costume and of the setting for the picture. It conveys an image of Henry's personal strength and of his royal power and majesty. The same direct, uncompromising gaze is apparent in his eyes as can be seen in the portrait of 'Young King Henry VIII' (provided on the CD).

Already gaining a great deal of weight on account of his lavish lifestyle, here Henry is shown as a large and imposing figure and appears a strong personality, well accustomed to exerting his authority. His royal status is evident in the richly embroidered clothes and regalia he wears. Feathers of the highest quality and furs of all descriptions were used to decorate his hats and coats. Gold thread and jewels were used in his costumes and were faithfully captured by the artist, who used real gold for the decoration and jewels in his portraits to achieve an effect of maximum realism.

Discussing the portrait

▶ Ask the children what kind of picture this is, and discuss whether they have seen it before. Explain that it is possibly the most famous of Henry VIII's portraits, and how it is frequently used for all kinds of purposes, such as the covers of books. Explain to the class how this picture has come to be one of the key images of the Tudor period for most people.

▶ Look again at Henry's expression. Talk about the significance of his gaze. What words could be used to describe his look; what does it tell us about him as a person?

▶ Find volunteers to give sentences describing Henry's clothes. Ask the class to suggest adjectives to describe the clothes and add these to the sentences already suggested.

Activities

▶ Help the children locate the date of this portrait on the timeline of Henry VIII's life.

▶ Find out about Holbein, the artist, including other portraits he painted.

▶ Provide the children with collage materials to re-create this picture. Display the children's work.

▶ Give the children a written description of Henry made at the time (see photocopiable page 32), and compare this with their own impressions. Ask them to underline the main descriptive words in the written account. They can then compare these words with those they themselves suggested.

▶ Provide time for the children to work in pairs at the computer to print off words and phrases to describe Henry in this pose, using different font sizes, styles and colours.

▶ Investigate further detail and information about Henry's life. Challenge the children to find out about his character as well as the things he did.

▶ Write a class description of Henry, based on his appearance in this portrait. Compare the description produced with the contemporary one on photocopiable page 32.

Catherine of Aragon

Catherine of Aragon was born a princess, the daughter of Ferdinand and Isabella of Spain. This portrait was painted by Michel Sittow in about 1500. At the time, she would have been about 14 or 15 years old.

At three Catherine was betrothed to Prince Arthur, Henry's older brother. The betrothal and marriage was intended to ensure a successful alliance between England and Spain. However, Arthur died only six months after the marriage. To maintain the alliance Henry then married Catherine in 1509, when Henry was 17 and Catherine was probably about 23. Shortly after their marriage, Catherine's first child was stillborn. This was a great disappointment, but it was soon followed by the birth of Prince Henry, but the baby died after only 52 days. Catherine then had a miscarriage, followed by another short-lived son, but in 1516, she gave birth to a daughter named Mary. Mary was to be Catherine's only surviving child and later become Queen Mary I (see 'Queen Mary I' provided on this CD).

Henry needed a son to provide a male heir. However, it was beginning to appear increasingly unlikely that the ageing Catherine would be able to produce one. This was to be the beginning of Henry's 'Great Matter'. Henry became convinced that his failure to produce a male heir to the throne was a sign of God's disapproval. He believed that his marriage was not a true one, since he had married the widow of his brother. Henry, who had great respect for Catherine, tried to persuade her to become a nun. Catherine refused, and after two years of argument with the Pope about a possible divorce, Henry appointed Thomas Cranmer as Archbishop of Canterbury. Cranmer declared the marriage annulled in 1533. Catherine was then sent to live in various castles away from the Court and was separated from her daughter. She died in 1536.

Discussing the portrait

▶ Discuss the kind of picture this is. Explain that it is a portrait by a famous artist of a Spanish princess who was the first wife of Henry VIII.

▶ Ask how old the children think she is here (about 14 or 15).

▶ Talk about the impression created by this picture. Ask what kind of person Catherine appears to be, for example, composed and confident of her position as a Spanish Princess.

▶ Encourage the children to suggest words to describe Catherine, and make a list of these for later use.

▶ Talk about the style and colour of her costume, for example the darkness and plainness of her dress. Discuss what this might suggest about Catherine or about the people who brought her up as a child.

▶ Tell the class about the situation that led to the marriage and then the divorce, for example Henry's need for a strong ally; his need for a male heir to the throne.

▶ Talk about the meaning of the word *divorce*. Explain how Henry always respected Catherine, even when he had divorced her.

Activities

▶ Remind the children of the date of this portrait and help them locate it on the timeline of Henry VIII's life (see photocopiable page 30). Note when Henry married Catherine and when he divorced her. Ask the children to calculate how long they were married.

▶ Discuss the problems that faced Henry and led to his divorce and make a list together with the class of all the advantages and disadvantages of the divorce. Explain that this issue became what Henry called in his own words, his 'Great Matter'.

▶ Compare Catherine's portrait with that of other ladies of the court in Tudor times and note the striking differences between how they dressed and looked, for example Anne Boleyn (provided on the CD). Explain how at the time members of the court thought that Catherine was old-fashioned.

▶ Take on the role of Catherine of Aragon yourself and encourage the children to devise and ask you questions.

▶ Provide materials for the children to make simple tapestries either in pairs or small groups, to show the portrait of Catherine of Aragon.

Europe in Tudor times

This map shows some of the major powers in Western Europe during the Tudor period. At that time Scotland and Ireland were independent nations in their own right, and while Ireland was largely Catholic, Scotland was partly Catholic and partly Protestant. It was during the reign of Henry VIII that England became a Protestant power. Henry VIII broke with Rome on account of his divorce from Catherine of Aragon. He declared the Church of England to be independent of interference from Rome, and made himself its head, thus providing himself the opportunity to marry Anne Boleyn legally in the eyes of the church. Henry used his new powers as head of the Church of England to attack Roman Catholicism, and ordered all the monasteries to be closed. Monuments, statues and vast numbers of books in ancient libraries were also destroyed as part of this 'dissolution' of the monasteries.

These events led to great enmity between England and Spain, since not only had Henry cast aside a Spanish princess, but he had also broken faith with the Catholic Church. Catholicism was still the only religion to be accepted in all the southern European nations at that time, such as Spain, Portugal and France. These three were all powerful and potentially serious rivals to English power within Europe. The Netherlands, also shown here, was divided. The Southern Netherlands were Catholic, while the North became Protestant. At times, the Netherlands became a useful ally for England.

Discussing the map

▶ Ask the children what part of the world this map shows.

▶ Find volunteers to read out the names of the countries. Point out the other words next to each name, for example *Protestant* and *Catholic*, and ask the children if they know what these words refer to. Explain the meaning of the two words and talk about what this meant for the different countries of Europe at the time, for example they disagreed with each other about religion.

▶ Ask the children which countries they think might go to war against each other because of their different beliefs, and because of their proximity, for example England and France. Explain that England and France did go to war regularly.

▶ Explain the meaning of the words *ally* and *alliance*.

▶ Tell the class that Henry wanted an alliance with another Protestant power. He could not seek an alliance with Protestants in Scotland however, because of the traditional rivalry between Scotland and England. Explain that Henry had to look towards the Germanic countries therefore for allies, because these were Protestant.

Activities

▶ Set the children the task of writing their own definitions of what is meant by *Protestant* and *Catholic*. (Catholics remained loyal to the Pope in Rome and continued to take the Catholic communion; Protestants were members of any Christian church which had cut itself off from the Roman Catholic communion. These were initially the Germanic countries who accepted the reforms of Martin Luther. Later, other churches, such as the Church of England, were Protestant.)

▶ Provide resources in the form of books and selected websites and set the children the task of finding out about the Pope at that time and about Martin Luther.

▶ Challenge the children to find out about other European countries at the time, and what their religions were, for example Italy, Denmark, Sweden, Norway, and so on. They can then add this information to their maps.

Anne Boleyn

This portrait, by an unknown artist of the English School, was painted in 1534. It shows Anne wearing the characteristic 'B' (for Boleyn) pendant. Although in this portrait she is dressed quite demurely, Anne had a reputation at court of being very fashionable. She tended to prefer the very modern French style of costume, and here wears the French bonnet of latest design. It was considered by some at the time to be rather daring in the way it was cut back to reveal a great deal of her hair. The portrait shows how Anne was dark and elegant in her appearance, rather than pretty in the accepted way at the time. She seems serious here, but capable of humour, and appears intelligent and elegant.

Anne Boleyn was born around 1500 and as a teenager lived in France for a number of years attending the queen at the French court. During her stay in France, Anne learned to speak French fluently and enjoyed French clothes, poetry and music. She was witty, well educated and cultured and although she was considered only moderately pretty, on her arrival at the English court to attend the queen, Henry clearly decided that he wanted her for his mistress. At first to those at court, Anne seemed just like any other mistress, but in 1527, Henry began to seek an annulment of his marriage to Catherine.

Henry secretly married Anne in 1533. In May, Archbishop Cranmer officially proclaimed that the marriage of Henry and Catherine was invalid and plans for Anne's coronation began. In 1533 Princess Elizabeth was born. There was, of course, disappointment and Anne knew that she must produce a son. After two miscarriages, Anne knew that her failure to produce a living male heir was a threat to her own life, especially since the king had developed an interest in another lady at court, Jane Seymour. In 1536, the queen was arrested at Greenwich and charged with adultery, incest and plotting to murder the king, who was genuinely outraged at her behaviour. In May of that year, she was beheaded at the Tower of London.

Discussing the portrait

▶ Ask the children if they have seen a portrait like this before. Can they guess who it is? Is there a clue?

▶ Ask if they think she looks like an important lady, and why they think this.

▶ Explain that this is Anne Boleyn, the second wife of Henry VIII. Tell the class about the problems Henry faced over the divorce from Catherine in order to marry Anne.

▶ Find out if any of the children know the name of Anne's child – Elizabeth, later to become Queen Elizabeth I.

▶ Encourage the children to look closely at the picture and think of words to describe Anne. What do they think she may have been like as a person; what clues are there?

▶ Explain that Anne was very up to date with fashions and how she liked French styles. Tell the class about her upbringing in France, which would have been different from English and Spanish traditions known at the court at the time.

▶ Ask why they think Henry VIII decided that he preferred Anne to Catherine. If they find this difficult to discuss explain how she was educated differently in the French court, and how her tastes were like Henry's; she liked music and literature and enjoyed the jokes, dancing, games and fun of the court.

Activities
See 'Katherine Parr', below.

Jane Seymour

This portrait of Jane Seymour was painted by Hans Holbein, probably shortly before her marriage to the king. The painting seems to confirm written accounts about her personality. She appears calm and composed, and also rather serious. Clearly of noble lineage, she is dressed elaborately in fashionable headdress, highly decorative, bejewelled clothes and wears the typically heavy Tudor jewellery. The woollen shawl or stole she wears over her arms, although likely to be expensive, also gives her a slightly 'homely' appearance.

Jane was born in about 1509, and married Henry VIII in 1536, the same year as the execution of Anne Boleyn. Before her marriage to Henry, Jane waited on Anne Boleyn at court, where Henry will have noticed her. Within 24 hours of Anne Boleyn's execution, Jane Seymour and Henry VIII were betrothed, and they married shortly afterwards. The birth of Prince Edward also followed swiftly. Jane attended her son's christening, although she was weak. She died two weeks after her son was born and only a year after her marriage. Jane was the only one of Henry's six wives to be eventually buried with him. Some think that Henry considered her to have been his only true wife. He did not remarry for some years after her death. (Although perhaps the trouble his ministers experienced finding a suitable fourth wife because of his reputation was more likely a reason for the delay than grief.)

Discussing the portrait
▶ Explain who this is to the class, and tell them that she is Henry VIII's third wife. Tell them about how he married her as soon as Anne Boleyn had been executed.

▶ Talk about why this was, and what had gone wrong with his relationship with Anne. For example, Anne was a very firm Protestant, and Henry still had some regard for the Catholic faith, in which he had been brought up. Anne also had a tendency to speak out of turn and contradict him in front of the court, which Henry did not like. She had annoyed him a great deal, especially when it was said that she had made other friends instead of Henry.

▶ Explain how Jane was pleased to have gained the king's attention, however, and to eventually marry him. Ask the children if they can give some reasons why this was, for example she would become Queen; become rich and famous; she might have a son to be heir to the throne; it would be good for her family, and so on.

▶ Talk about the possible danger she might be in and the disadvantages of being married to Henry, for example he might change his mind about her; her children may not survive.

▶ Consider how she looks in this portrait, and ask the children to give as many words to describe Jane's appearance as they can. Write down these words for future use. Ask the children to describe what kind of person they think Jane was from looking at her portrait.

▶ Explain how some historians think that she was Henry's favourite wife, and discuss reasons why this was, for example she bore him a son; she was kind and caring; she died before he could become tired of her.

Activities
See 'Katherine Parr', below.

Anne of Cleves

The split from Rome meant that England might be attacked by a number of Catholic powers. Therefore, Henry and his ministers began to look at the possibility of forming an alliance through marriage with a Protestant power, such as Cleves, where the Duke could be a useful ally. Henry sent painters to bring him images of eligible women in foreign courts. Consequently, Holbein was sent to Germany to paint Anne of Cleves' portrait (the duke's daughter) in 1539. When Henry saw the portrait of Anne (born in 1515) he decided to marry her and they married in January 1540. They divorced in July of that same year.

There is little evidence here that Anne was as ugly as many accounts claim, although some argue that Holbein was under instructions to produce a flattering portrait. In this portrait, she is composed and appears elegant, wearing an elaborate lace headdress, decorated with jewels. She wears heavy flowing robes possibly of velvet, her dress intricately embroidered and the detail at the neckline picked out with more jewels. Her cross is very evident among the other necklaces. It may be significant that more is made of her dress than her face and her eyes are slightly downcast.

By the time of the marriage, Henry had already decided to get out of the arrangement. Anne's upbringing in Cleves had trained her in domestic skills rather than the music and other courtly skills that Henry enjoyed. Also, Henry did not like his new bride. He wanted to end the marriage because of his personal dislike of Anne, but there were now also political reasons. The Duke of Cleves was threatening war with the Holy Roman Empire and Henry did not wish to be involved. Henry had by now also become attracted to Catherine Howard, another young lady at the Court. Anne agreed to the divorce and after the marriage had been dissolved, she moved away from court and lived quietly until her death in 1557.

Discussing the portrait

▶ Explain to the children that this is a portrait of Anne of Cleves, Henry VIII's fourth wife. Talk about how she was from a German state, called Cleves, and how she was the daughter of the Duke and who he was.

▶ Encourage the children to look carefully at the portrait and find clues that tell us that she was an important person in her own right.

▶ Look at her face and her expression and discuss what this might tell us about her personality, for example she seems serious and very 'correct' in her pose.

▶ Discuss whether this kind of person would have appealed to Henry.

▶ Explain to the class why the portrait was painted, and how Henry married Anne on the basis of seeing the portrait, before he had even met her in person.

▶ Talk about Henry's reaction to Anne, and how he said she was ugly.

▶ Talk about whether the painting may not have been a true likeness of Anee and reasons why.

▶ Tell the class the story about Anne (see photocopiable page 31). Discuss the fact that Henry might not have liked her personality as well as her appearance, because she did not share his sense of humour or laugh at his jokes, as he expected she should.

Activities

See 'Katherine Parr', below.

Catherine Howard

No known portrait of Catherine Howard has been positively identified. However, this portrait, painted by Sarah, Countess of Essex in 1825, is a reproduction of a painting which may show Catherine around the time of her marriage. It shows a young woman of high position, wearing the fashionable French headdress of the time, along with the heavy jewellery and embroidered, bejewelled clothes of the age.

Catherine, or Kathryn, Howard was born in 1521. First cousin to Anne Boleyn, she came to court as a lady-in-waiting to Anne of Cleves. 16 days after he was free of Anne, Henry married Catherine, on July 28, 1540. Henry was 49 and the bride 19.

Less than a year into their marriage, rumours of her infidelity began. Catherine liked the fun of the court and enjoyed showing off her looks and her fashionable clothes. She made friends easily, especially with the young men at the court. Catherine, young and inexperienced in court politics, appointed one of her admirers as her personal secretary, making matters worse. By November 1541, there was enough evidence against the queen that Archbishop Cranmer informed the king of Catherine's misconduct. At first, Henry did not believe the accusations. Eventually sufficient evidence was gathered about the queen's behaviour to bring charges against her, and she was executed and laid to rest near her cousin Anne Boleyn in the chapel at the Tower of London in 1542.

Discussing the portrait

▶ Explain to the class that this may be a portrait of Catherine Howard, Henry VIII's fifth wife. We cannot be certain that it is Catherine, since there has been no positive identification of a portrait of her. Discuss why there are no known portraits of Catherine Howard; what might have happened to them?

▶ Discuss the features of the portrait, and how we can tell that this was an important person. Ask the children to find all the clues they can for this.

▶ Discuss the surrounding to the portrait. What can the children see below the picture, and why do they think these items are there? Discuss whether these things are likely to have been placed around a portrait that was made while Catherine was still alive. Discuss how and when they may have been added. Finally, consider why they might have been added, and whether this suggests the portrait is a real one or not.

▶ Encourage the children to look closely at Catherine and identify features of her costume. Discuss the style of clothes she liked to wear, for example very fashionable and flattering; jewellery and bejewelled gowns.

▶ Look at Catherine herself, and consider what her portrait tells us about her character and what she was like at the time, for example she was very young; she liked to appear very attractive; she would have drawn attention to herself at court because of her fine clothes and modern headdress.

▶ Tell the children what happened to Catherine in the end.

Activities

See 'Katherine Parr', below.

Katherine Parr

An unknown artist painted this portrait, identified as that of Katherine Parr. Katherine Parr was born in 1512, she married Henry in 1543 and died in 1548. Katherine, the daughter of Thomas Parr, a modest country squire, was the last of the ageing king's wives. Katherine's widowed mother encouraged the education of all her children, including the girls, and this may have set the model for Katherine's future involvement in the education of her stepchildren, Mary, Elizabeth and Edward.

Once married, Katherine must have acted as a nurse to the now sick king. She managed to soothe the king's temper and became a mother figure to his family. Katherine arranged for the best tutors for the children and encouraged them in their learning. She outlived Henry, who died January 28, 1547. Katherine herself died in 1548 after giving birth to a daughter from a subsequent marriage.

Discussing the portrait

▶ Explain to the class that this is a portrait of Katherine Parr, Henry VIII's sixth wife.

▶ Discuss the features of the portrait, and how we can tell that this was an important person. Ask the children to find all the clues they can for this.

▶ Explain that Henry married Katherine when he was getting old and sick. Tell them how he was quite ill by this time, and very bad-tempered. Explain how Katherine Parr was like a nurse to him and took on the job of taking care of him until he died.

▶ Encourage the children to look closely at Katherine and identify features of her costume. Discuss the style of clothes she liked to wear, for example jewellery and rich gowns.

▶ Look at Katherine herself, and consider what her portrait tells us about her character and what she was like at the time, for example she was much younger than Henry; she was quite serious and caring; she looks very honest and direct; she had the poise and manner of a queen.

Activities

▶ Remind the children of the dates when Henry married each queen and when he divorced or had them executed or when they died. Help them to locate these dates on a blank timeline of Henry VIII's reign. Can the children calculate how long he was married to each queen? To whom was he married the longest? Which was his shortest marriage?

▶ Tell the class about the situation that led to so many marriages and then the divorces and executions, for example Henry's need for a strong ally in another country; his need for a male heir to the throne; his own pride and vanity. Discuss the problems that this created for Henry and his advisers.

▶ Make a picture gallery, using collage, tapestry or paints and encourage the children to write captions or descriptions about each of the queens.

▶ Give the children sentence starters for each of Henry wives, for example *Henry VIII married Catherine of Aragon because…* and ask them to complete them.

▶ Give the children large poster paper and ask them to design proclamations issued by the royal palace announcing each of the king's marriages. The class could be divided into groups to work on the posters.

▶ Choose six children to take on the roles of the queens and encourage the children to devise and ask questions of each one.

▶ Make a class book about Henry VIII and his queens. As a conclusion to the book, get the children to write their own explanations for Henry's succession of marriages.

King Edward VI

Born in 1537, Edward VI was sickly throughout his short life. Henry VIII died happy in the belief that he had finally secured the succession with a male heir. However, Edward, aged nine on his accession, survived only until 1553, dying at the age of 16. He had never even assumed full responsibility in his role as monarch. His reign is characterised by unrest caused by his senior advisors vying for power. Before Edward died of tuberculosis, Dudley, Duke of Northumberland and Lord Protector, in the king's name persuaded him to sign 'Letters Patent', excluding both his half-sisters, Mary and Elizabeth, from the succession, in favour of Lady Jane Grey, who was married to Dudley's son, Guildford Dudley, and who only reigned for nine days.

This portrait, painted by Guillim Stretes (also known as William Scrots) in 1551, shows many of Edward's significant characteristics. Here he is about 14 or 15 years old. Despite the fact that the artist has cleverly created a pose reminiscent of the famous Holbein portrait of his father (see 'King Henry VIII when older', provided on the CD), and although Edward is dressed in a similar way, Edward himself does not resemble his powerful father. Instead he appears slight and pale, almost timid. He has not been able, despite everyone's best efforts, to assume here the arrogant, assertive persona of his father, and was unable to achieve this during his time as king.

Discussing the portrait

▶ Explain to the class that this is a portrait of King Edward VI – Henry VIII's son who became king upon his father's death. Explain that he was very young when he became king and was advised by a 'lord protector'.

▶ Ask the children to study Edward's costume carefully and note its features.

▶ Encourage the children to look closely at Edward's face and his expression. Discuss whether we can tell what sort of person he was from this picture.

▶ Make a list of words suggested by the children in describing his character and appearance.

Activities

▶ Look at the timeline of the Tudor period (photocopiable page 29) and discuss how long Edward was on the throne. Encourage the children to work out the number of years he reigned. Ask them to make a list of all the disadvantages he would have faced when he came to the throne, for example his age; the squabbling among his advisers; the religious problems, and so on.

▶ Compare the portrait with Holbein's portrait of Henry VIII ('King Henry VIII when older', provided on this CD). Compare the two portraits and discuss why there are such similarities between them. Having noted the similarities, ask the children to point out things that are different, for example the age, size and manner of Edward compared with his father.

▶ Provide the children with materials to make a collage of Edward's portrait and place this next to their version of the portrait of Henry VIII.

▶ Collect useful materials, books and suitable extracts from websites for the children to use in their research into Edward's life. Set them some questions to answer in their research, such as *What did Edward do all day when he first became king? Who was in charge of the country at first and what was his title? What part did Edward play in running the country when he grew older?*

▶ Provide the children with information about the famous artists and portrait painters of the time, such as Holbein, Sittow, Stretes and Moro, and encourage them to read about these and remember their names. Set them the task of finding out about other famous portrait painters at other times in history from library resources.

Queen Mary I

This portrait of Queen Mary I was painted in 1554 by Antonio Moro (also known as Antonis Mor). Moro worked as court artist at the courts of Charles V and Phillip II, Mary's Spanish husband. He is renowned as one of the finest portrait artists of his age. Moro has managed to capture in Mary's face, the effects of a life of intense suffering, while at the same time, representing her majestic and somewhat arrogant pose. Mary looks very regal, seated on her throne. She is evidently of very high birth, as is indicated by her costume. She wears large, heavy jewels and an ornate headdress. Her coat is well designed with an unusual high collar, while her dress is intricately embroidered, with lace collar and cuffs. She holds the red rose of the Tudors in her right hand.

As the daughter of Catherine of Aragon (see page 9), Mary experienced very unhappy times – including the upheaval of her parents' divorce and the execution of two stepmothers. Her face, to some extent, shows the horrors through which she has lived. There is also apparent a harshness and tension in her pose and gaze. Mary looks hard and determined. As queen, she set herself against her father's Protestant church, imprisoning her stepsister, Elizabeth, and conducting a campaign of terror and murder at the Protestants.

Discussing the portrait

▶ Look at the 'Tudor timeline' (see photocopiable page 29) with the class and then point out that this portrait is of Queen Mary I. Explain when it was painted and by whom.

▶ Ask the children why they think Mary was painted by such a famous artist, for example she was Queen of England and also the wife of King Phillip II of Spain, who was very rich and powerful.

▶ Suggest the children talk about their first impressions of the picture; what does it immediately suggest to them? For example, she is very important, sitting on a throne; she is perhaps quite stern or strict.

▶ Encourage the children to look more closely at Mary's costume and to pick out the important features about it. Note the large jewels she wears and talk about the names of all these items, such as *necklace*, *pendant*.

▶ Ask the children if there is anything special or unusual about this portrait, for example the rose in Mary's hand. Ask if they can work out why she is holding this, for example it is the Tudor Rose – the symbol of the Tudor dynasty.

▶ Finally, ask the children to look closely at Mary's face and her expression. They need to think of words to describe her character based on what they can see in the portrait. Make a note of these for use in future writing.

Activities

▶ Locate the reign of Queen Mary I on the 'Tudor timeline' (photocopiable page 29). Discuss the length of her reign and challenge the children to work out how long she was on the throne.

▶ Research into the affairs of Mary's reign yourself and set up a hot-seating activity where you yourself take on Mary's character. Set the class the task of interviewing you in the role of newspaper reporters. They then write short newspaper reports about the things you divulge, such as your decision to burn Protestants at the stake and to imprison your half-sister Elizabeth in the Tower of London.

▶ Divide the class into two halves, those who favour Mary and those who do not. Initiate a debate about the reign of Mary and whether she was a good or bad queen, nominating a pair from each 'side' as spokespeople. At the end of the debate, conduct a vote to find out the majority opinion.

Queen Elizabeth I

This portrait of Elizabeth I was painted in 1585 by Nicholas Hilliard. It is known as the 'Ermine Portrait' because of the small ermine resting on the queen's sleeve. Its fur has been painted to look like the ermine used in garments, with the characteristic dark triangular marks. Although the fur is naturally plain white, the darker tufts are added from the tail when the fur is made into garments. Queen Elizabeth I had numerous portraits painted showing herself in many different scenes. Most portraits are like this one, focusing on the grandeur of the queen and emphasising her fine features, high forehead, immaculate hair and sumptuous clothes. She wears here an extensive ruff of lace, with matching lace cuffs, and an exquisitely bejewelled crown. Her gown is of rich fabric, innovatively embroidered and with jewelled fastenings.

The production of portraits like this one was all part of the Tudor propaganda campaign to raise the monarchy in the esteem of the common people. This was necessary because Elizabeth's reign was at times very unsettled, particularly for many poor working people, with continual attempts by claimants to the throne to overthrow her and riots among the population. Despite a growing merchant class and increasing wealth for a few, the period was one of considerable unrest, due to poor harvests, unemployment and massive inflation. The strongest and most dangerous threat to Elizabeth's monarchy came from Mary Queen of Scots, a Catholic queen in her own right, who had a real claim to the throne. After keeping her prisoner in the Tower of London for many years, Elizabeth was finally forced to order her execution, following rumours of yet another rebellious plot. Another worry was the issue of the succession. Elizabeth steadfastly refused to marry, no doubt after witnessing the treatment of the royal wives during the reign of her father. Instead she ruled alone and left no child to inherit the throne. Despite these problems, Elizabeth did maintain her hold on the throne and lived to a healthy old age, finally dying in 1603.

Discussing the portrait

▶ Ask the children what their first impressions of this portrait are. What does it suggest about the person who has had the portrait made?

▶ Ask if they recognise the sitter, and if they have seen pictures like this before. Talk about what the picture is known as and when it was painted. Talk about the ermine and how it is still used to trim royal costumes and is a sign of nobility. Discuss why Elizabeth has an ermine in her portrait. Explain that Elizabeth was at the height of her power.

▶ Get the children to comment on her costume, noting the descriptive vocabulary they use.

▶ Point out her pose, the position of her hands and her expression, and discuss what these features suggest about her. Encourage the children to study her expression carefully and then to suggest what they think she was like as a person.

Activities

▶ Help the children to locate the period of Elizabeth's reign on the 'Tudor timeline' (photocopiable page 29). Challenge them to work out the length of her reign and point out how hers was the longest reign of all the Tudors. In fact it is one of the longest in the history of England.

▶ Ask the children to search for further information about the reign of Elizabeth. Set them the task of working in pairs to make notes on Elizabeth herself; her friends; her enemies, such as Mary Queen of Scots; the heroes of the reign, such as Sir Francis Drake; and the key events of the reign, such as the Armada. Using the notes the children have made, arrange for them to produce a presentation, wall display or class book about the information they have found.

▶ Make a large outline figure of Elizabeth and use a variety of delicate fabrics to create an impression of the rich clothes she wore, such as the gown in the ermine portrait.

▶ Talk about why Elizabeth did not marry, and encourage the children to work out a variety of reasons why this was. For example, she would have lost her power and authority; she did not meet anyone she wanted to marry; she did not have to ally herself to any particular faction and so on. Suggest the children make a series of simple sketches or cartoons of Elizabeth, with speech bubbles explaining why she did not want to marry, from her own point of view.

▶ Set the more able writers the task of writing a story about Elizabeth.

The *Mary Rose*

This modern painting of the *Mary Rose* by William Bishop was commissioned in the 1980s by the *Mary Rose* Trust. The oil painting shows in detail and as accurately as we know, how the ship originally looked. It is entitled, 'The Warship *Mary Rose* leaving Portsmouth Harbour – Summer 1545'. The *Mary Rose*, which came to be Henry's favourite warship, was named after his younger sister, Mary, and after the Tudor Rose. Built in 1510, soon after Henry acceded to the throne, the *Mary Rose* was a large ship, advanced for the time. She was about 400 tons and, from documentary evidence, appears to have been built in Portsmouth and fitted out with guns in London. No expense seems to have been spared in fitting her out since she was to be Henry VIII's flagship. She needed a crew of about 410 men to sail her.

When Henry went to war with France in 1512, the *Mary Rose* was the flagship of the fleet. During the battle, the *Mary Rose* inflicted considerable damage on the flagship of the French fleet. She was later involved in several conflicts, in 1522, and again in 1543. Unfortunately, following repairs and alterations made, apparently to requirements specified by Henry himself, the *Mary Rose* capsized and sank while setting out to engage in battle once more with the French in 1545, drowning nearly all her crew.

Discussing the painting

▶ Ask the children what kind of picture this is – is it a painting or a photograph?

▶ Discuss whether it looks old-fashioned or modern, and during the discussion draw the children's attention to the fact that the ship is a very old-fashioned one, but the painting is modern. Discuss how we know both these things, for example the ship has sails and tall decks in the Tudor style; the painting is very detailed and realistic, unlike paintings at the time which were very stylised and 'flat' looking, or two-dimensional.

▶ Ask the children whether they think this is a large ship. Discuss what clues can tell us this. Talk about how many crew members would be needed to sail her.

▶ Discuss the number of masts, sails and decks.

▶ Talk about what kind of ship she was – a warship – and ask the children to look for evidence of this, for example the guns.

▶ Explain that this ship was called the *Mary Rose* and that she was Henry VIII's flagship, the most important ship in the fleet. Also tell the class about the new design of the ship which meant she could have guns which fired sideways, that is broadside, a new idea at the time.

▶ Finally, explain to the class what happened to the *Mary Rose* in the end, and how she has been recovered from the seabed. She is now on display in Portsmouth.

Activities

▶ Help the children to place the key events in the history of the *Mary Rose* onto the class timeline. Encourage them to work out how long the *Mary Rose* sailed as the king's flagship.

▶ Find out about the many thousands of artefacts that were discovered in the wreckage – see 'Cannon from the *Mary Rose*', 'Navigational instruments from the *Mary Rose*', 'Tableware found on the *Mary Rose*' and 'Domestic items found on the *Mary Rose*' (provided on this CD).

▶ Provide children with materials to make their own detailed drawing or painting of the ship, such as watercolours or pastels.

▶ If possible, organise a visit to the *Mary Rose* in Portsmouth or a similar ship, or to a replica of one, such as the Golden Hinde in Southwark, London.

▶ Provide word cards for the children to use and set them the task of writing a newspaper report about the sinking of the *Mary Rose*, following the fitting of new guns in 1545. Ask them to make the report a front-page piece, with a large headline.

Cannon from the *Mary Rose*

In 1982, the wreck of the *Mary Rose* was discovered and raised after more than 400 years on the seabed. The raising of the *Mary Rose*, an historic event in itself, brought to light a vast amount of detailed evidence about ships and life on board in Tudor times, in the form of the ship itself and the many artefacts discovered on board. Among these many objects, were nearly all of the heavy guns used on the ship.

This is one of the bronze broadside guns found on the starboard side of the main deck. There would also have been some iron guns on this deck. The original gun can be seen in this photograph, on a reconstructed carriage. The carriage would have been made from elm wood with four solid wheels. It would have been used to pull back the gun from the side of the ship for cleaning and reloading. The gun would have been loaded from the front and would have fired iron shot over long distances. They could damage the hull and rigging of enemy ships, as well as killing the crew. Each bronze gun was individually made, and was highly decorated and inscribed. They represented the power and wealth of the Tudor monarchy as well as being a very effective weapon.

Discussing the photograph

▶ Ask the children what this is and where they think it has come from. Discuss the raising of the *Mary Rose* and explain that it is one of the guns, or cannon, from her deck.

▶ Talk about what these cannon were made from, for example either iron or bronze, and discuss what they fired as shot.

▶ Encourage the children to look again more closely at the detail on the cannon, and how carefully it is decorated. Discuss why the children think this was, for example it was to show the power of the king's ship.

▶ Discuss the trolley or carriage that the cannon rests on. Ask if the children think this was probably found with the *Mary Rose*, or is it likely to have been made since. Discuss why this is (the wood would have rotted away).

▶ Talk about how this type of carriage would have been used with the cannon in battles on the *Mary Rose*, and ask the children why the gun needed a carriage, for example it was extremely heavy; it needed to be moved to load it and clean it.

Activities

▶ Look back to the picture of 'The *Mary Rose*' (provided on the CD) and try to work out roughly how many cannon there might have been on board.

▶ Provide books and non-fiction resources for the children to investigate the use of guns on ships in Tudor times and later periods in history. Ask them to make notes and then to talk to the class about their findings at the end of the lesson.

▶ Provide the children with drawing materials and ask them to make detailed drawings of the cannon and label the different parts, for example muzzle, barrel.

▶ Use reclaimed materials to make models of the cannon. In design and technology, the children can attempt to make carriages that will wheel back and forth.

Navigational instruments from the *Mary Rose*

Among the 25 000 artefacts found on the *Mary Rose* were early navigational instruments like these. Shown in this picture are: a pair of dividers, a protractor and a sundial and its lid. The Tudors carried sundials and used them in much the same way as a pocket watch. Not having the clockwork timepiece of later ages, the Tudors used the position of the Sun, which they could check with their sundial, to work out the time of day. The dividers and protractor would have aided mariners in plotting their routes and in working out their position at sea on large maps.

At this time, sea travel was very hazardous, not least because the skill of navigation was still in its infancy. It was not until many years later that navigators worked out both latitude and longitude, because they had no reliable type of clock that could be used at sea. However, using instruments like the ones in this photograph, they could work out how far they had travelled, but they were unable to work out how far north or south they were. This meant that they were unable to accurately pinpoint their position on a map. Needless to say, ships frequently went hundreds of miles off course, sometimes running into rocks and sinking because they were unable to navigate with sufficient accuracy to avoid such dangers.

Discussing the photograph

▶ Ask the children to look at the objects in the photograph and to see if they remind them of any modern things, for example the protractor and dividers.

▶ Ask who they think may have used them and what for.

▶ Discuss what they were, for example navigational instruments.

▶ Talk about the meaning of the word *navigation* and how early navigators had to use the Sun to find out where they were on the ocean.

▶ Discuss why navigation is very difficult at sea, for example no landmarks. Also consider why navigation is so important, and why it was especially important in the past. For example, if ships got lost they would run out of food and water; they may run aground or hit rocks and be wrecked. Explain that this did, in fact, happen a great deal.

▶ Talk about why it was difficult to navigate precisely when using these old tools, for example it was difficult to take accurate readings when the ship was constantly moving.

▶ Look at the tiny discs. Explain that these are parts of a sundial, a small box and a lid. Tell the children that the Tudors used these rather like we use a watch today. They would use their tiny sundial to find the position of the Sun and from that, work out what time of day it was.

Activities

▶ Find pictures of other navigational instruments, such as the astrolabe and compass. Have the children make observational drawings of these. Talk and write about how they were used.

▶ Make a collection of pictures of old maps used at this time (there are a great many on the Internet). Ask the children to note how much the Tudors knew about the world, by looking at their maps.

▶ Make some models of these instruments and see if it is possible to work out the Sun's position using them. Show the children how to use a compass and compare a modern compass with a Tudor version.

▶ Look at a sundial or a picture of one, and consider how it is used to tell the time. Ask the children to record different times of day using these old pieces of equipment.

▶ If possible, find an extract from a film or broadcast which shows someone using the instruments, for example there is a good episode in the film of Columbus' voyage, *1492*.

Tableware found on the *Mary Rose*

This photograph shows some of the plates, spoons and containers for drinks that were discovered among the treasures of the *Mary Rose*. It is interesting to note that they are mostly made from pewter or wood. Wood was widely used to make all kinds of everyday objects in Tudor times because it was plentiful and cheap. Pewter, a soft metal with a silver finish, was also popular in Tudor times. This collection contains: a peppermill, wooden bowl, wicker-bound ceramic flask with a wooden plate behind it, pewter flagon, small pewter plate, wooden bowl (wooden spoon resting inside), large pewter plate, wooden stave-built tankard, pewter spoon and wooden spoon. It is interesting to note that the spoons had shorter handles than we are used to today.

It was not common for people to eat from a plate in Tudor times. Instead, most dishes would be served on a large plate placed in the middle of the table. The food would then be placed on trenchers of bread, and eaten from this, rather than from an individual plate. This is why many Tudor plates are much deeper than modern ones. They were designed to hold large quantities of food.

Domestic items found on the *Mary Rose*

This photograph provides a selection of some of the domestic items found on the *Mary Rose*. As well as plates, spoons and various vessels the collection includes interesting personal possessions such as an ear scoop, manicure set, weights and knife handles. There is also a comb and a tidy box for all these personal possessions to be kept in. The personal items are of particular interest in the way they show the care taken by more affluent Tudors in their appearance. These items also suggest that in many ways, life was remarkably similar to modern times.

Discussing the photographs

▶ Look at the two photographs of tableware and domestic items found on the wreckage of the *Mary Rose*. Ask the children to say what items they can recognise.

▶ Talk about how many of these things look similar to their modern equivalents.

▶ Ask the children what they think the items are made of, and how they think they were made. Note how the materials they were made from were different from materials used today. Explain why wood was popular.

▶ Discuss which items would have been used by the ordinary seamen, and which might have been for the officers and captain. For example, the wooden items are more likely to have been for the crew.

▶ Look at the size of the large plates or 'chargers'. Explain how food was served and eaten in Tudor times.

▶ Look at the wooden tankard and let the children guess what kind of drink it might have been used for.

▶ Discuss the personal items found on the Mary Rose. Ask the children which might be used today and which might not, for example the ear scoop. Discuss why not (health and safety). Talk about the similarities with modern-day possessions, and note how little life has changed in some respects.

Activities

▶ Ask the children to find out more about what food was eaten on board ship in Tudor times and how it was served and eaten.

▶ Ask the children to make observational drawings of some of the objects. If possible try to provide replicas of these items for them to handle.
▶ Hold a 'ship's dinner' in the form of a short drama or mime, in which the children re-enact a mealtime aboard the *Mary Rose*.
▶ Encourage the children to write the script for the piece they re-enacted above, using the correct terms for these utensils.

Greensleeves

Henry VIII was famed in Tudor times for his skill and love of music, enjoying the dances and songs of courtly life. There is little doubt that he will have composed tunes and songs to please the ladies he wished to admire him, and for some time it was thought that this famous melody was one of his compositions. It is now thought by most historians, however, that Henry did not compose the famous tune 'Greensleeves', and the idea has become one of legend. However, Henry was a skilled musician and is known to have played the harp, virginal, lute and organ at a high standard. He composed many pieces of music, among them a piece called 'Helas Madame'.

This piece was played on the broadly authentic instruments for the time: treble recorder, viola da gamba (a six-stringed instrument played between the legs rather like a cello) and archlute (a lute with two pegboxes).

Discussing the music

▶ Listen quietly to the music with the class. It is a short extract and may need to be repeated a few times.
▶ Ask the children if they have heard this music before. If they have, let them sing the next part of the tune.
▶ Talk about how it used to be thought that Henry VIII had written this tune. However, explain that now, it is known that he did not. Suggest to the children that the tune is probably very like those that Henry would have written, since he was a keen musician.
▶ Tell the class about the many instruments Henry played.
▶ Listen to the music again and talk about the instruments that are used. Does it sound like a modern version of the tune?

Activities

▶ Ask the children to find out about Tudor instruments and group them into different categories, such as strings, percussion, wind, and so on.
▶ Find examples of other Tudor music and play this to the class. Ask them to write their impressions and feelings about the music when they have listened to it.
▶ Explain how Henry VIII and especially his daughter, Elizabeth, liked to dance, and how there were many famous dances at the Tudor court. If possible, find examples of tunes for these dances, and teach the children some of the steps.
▶ If possible, invite some specialists in early music to play at the school and possibly to demonstrate some of the dances for the children.

NOTES ON THE PHOTOCOPIABLE PAGES

Word and sentence cards

PAGES 25–28

Specific types of vocabulary have been introduced on the word and sentence cards. These relate to the Tudors, government, describing people and connectives. Encourage the children to think of other appropriate words to add to those provided, in order to build up a word bank for the theme of the Tudors. They could include words encountered in their research, such as *warship*, *sailors*, *pewter*, in relation to discoveries from the *Mary Rose*. They could also use the cards in labelling displays and in writing simple and complex sentences to record what they have learned, for example sentences including the connective *because*, when explaining the king's reasons for marrying six times. They should also use the word cards as support in descriptive, factual and creative work and in writing discussions and arguments.

Activities

▶ Once you have made copies of the word and sentence cards, cut them out and laminate them, use them as often as possible when talking about the Tudors. They could be used for word games and spelling games, or to assist the less able readers to make up their own sentences or phrases.

▶ Add further vocabulary to the set of words, using those suggested by the children.

▶ Make displays of aspects of Tudor life and use word and sentence cards to label and describe them.

▶ Encourage the children to read the labels and sentences to yourself, adult helpers and visitors to the classroom.

▶ Encourage the children to use the words in stories and non-fiction writing as often as possible.

▶ Organise times during whole class plenaries to practise reading the sentence cards together. Follow up this activity with pairs of children reading the sentences. Check which words each child can read. Ask the children to create new sentences of their own.

▶ Add the words to the class word bank, and encourage the children to copy or write them frequently, for example when using writing or drawing frames or doing their own extended writing.

▶ Make word searches and crossword puzzles for the children to complete using specific sets of words related to the current topic, such as words to do with the monarchy.

▶ Make cloze procedure sheets omitting the words from the text. Encourage the children to write and spell the words without support.

▶ Devise 20 questions and 'hangman' games based on the word cards.

Tudor timeline
PAGE 29

This timeline shows all of the Tudor monarchs. Following the Battle of Bosworth and defeat of Richard III in 1485, Henry Tudor of Wales took over as king. A very prudent king, Henry carefully managed both the politics and the economy, building a secure foundation for his heir to inherit. He married Elizabeth of York, thus combining the competing Yorkist line of inheritance with his own and effectively bringing an end to the Wars of the Roses. His oldest son and heir, Arthur, died and it was his younger brother Henry who became king. Henry VIII's reign was characterised by his desire to have a son and to secure good foreign alliances. Edward succeeded his father. His short reign was dominated by those wishing to confirm England as a Protestant state and the reigns of both Mary and Elizabeth were similarly dominated by religious issues. First Mary attempted to re-establish the Catholic faith, and then her half-sister Elizabeth worked to reinstate Protestantism.

This timeline could be adapted for the classroom in the form of a long string which could be stretched across the classroom, to represent the distance in time covered by the Tudor period.

Discussing the timeline

▶ Ask the children if they know what is meant by the words *monarch*, *dynasty*, *house*, and explain that all of these words can be used to describe the Tudors.

▶ Explain how the dynasty began with Henry VII and ended with the death of Elizabeth I. Discuss why this happened, for example Elizabeth had no heir so the crown passed to another family, called the *Stuarts*.

▶ Look at the timeline and ensure the children understand how it is set out, for example the time progresses as we read from left to right. Explain how timelines can sometimes look different and need to be read in different directions. Check they understand by asking questions such as *Who was the first Tudor monarch? Who was the last?* and so on.

▶ Discuss the different dates with the class and ensure that each child understands the dating system, for example *Did Edward come to the throne before Henry VIII or after? Is 1533 before or after 1509? What century is 1558 in? In what century did Queen Elizabeth I die?*

▶ Challenge the children to work out how long each monarch reigned, and how long the Tudor family was on the throne of England.

Activities

▶ During shared writing time, compose a written account of the Tudor monarchs, explaining the order of succession and giving a brief account of why each monarch came to the throne.

▶ Challenge the children to design a timeline or family tree of their own.

▶ Adapt the timeline to create a large wall frieze to which the pictures (provided on the CD) could be added. Encourage the children to add pictures to the timeline as the topic progresses.

▶ Discuss the characters of each of the monarchs and talk about which one the children think did the most for Britain and which one they like best. Hold a vote and record the result as a bar chart to find out which is the most popular Tudor monarch in the class.

▶ Talk about why we remember so much about the Tudors, and why they are important to us. Ask the children to write a newspaper article about the death of the last of the Tudors and the reasons we will remember their dynasty.

Henry VIII timeline

PAGE 30

This timeline can be used to introduce children to the notion of chronology over a specific, recognisable span of time, in this case, the life of Henry VIII. The information it contains focuses mainly on the dates of Henry's marriages and the births of his children. It also includes references to the wars with France and the sinking of the Mary Rose. The timeline helps to emphasise how quickly Henry remarried on occasions when his previous wife had been divorced or executed. The timeline will be useful in discussions about the reasons for and the effects of Henry's decisions.

The kind of timeline shown here can also be useful at the end of a topic, for checking children's success in grasping ideas of sequence, chronology and, for those at that stage, understanding of the use of dates.

Discussing the timeline

▶ Ask the class at the beginning of the topic what they think this timeline shows. Explain that this line with dates and pictures represents the passing of time.

▶ Clarify what the dates on the timeline mean.

▶ Talk about the key events during the life of Henry VIII, and add more labels and events as appropriate.

▶ Use the stories and accounts of Henry and his wives, and the pictures provided on the CD to illustrate the discussion about the timeline.

Activities

▶ Make a class timeline using the timeline on the photocopiable as an example. Ask children to put on any other pictures or portraits from the period they find, in the appropriate places on the timeline. Build up a more detailed illustrated timeline as the topic progresses.

▶ Tell stories from the history of Tudor England and use the pictures from the CD when looking at the timeline.

▶ Give the children a blank timeline, or a section of the timeline, with either relevant dates or words and ask them to draw or paste on to it relevant pictures in the right places.

▶ Compare the different reasons for Henry's marriages and provide the children with a Venn diagram to sort out Henry's personal reasons and those reasons which were for the country. Some reasons overlap, such as the need for an heir to the throne.

Story of Anne of Cleves

PAGE 31

This story is based on real events that took place prior to the wedding of Henry VIII and Anne of Cleves. It helps to throw light onto Henry's sudden dislike of her. It is possible that it was as much her manner and behaviour, as her appearance, that displeased him. Additionally, she failed to flatter his sense of humour, a fatal mistake with a monarch used to having his own way at all times. It is also possible that the portrait Henry saw was not a very accurate likeness, since it was the custom at the time to tend to flatter important clients who had commissioned portraits.

Discussing the story

▶ Discuss whether Anne could have been a person easily shocked and frightened by Henry's behaviour.

▶ Ask the children if they think Anne was right to be annoyed at the king's behaviour.

▶ Ask what they would have done in those circumstances; would they have laughed at the king's joke?

▶ Talk about what light it throws on the character of Henry VIII, especially when he storms out of the room, declaring that he did not like her at all.

Activities

▶ Read the story to the class while showing them the portrait of 'Anne of Cleves' (provided on the CD). Discuss whether the portrait suggests that she is very strict and serious. Ask the children to think of words to describe the kind of person Anne seems to be in the portrait and the kind of person she is in the story. Compare the two sets of words to see if they give the same impression of her.

▶ Find the date of Anne's marriage to Henry on the class timeline. Look up when she was divorced, and talk about how Henry had already decided he did not like Anne even before they were married.

▶ Set one half of the class the task of writing the story of this incident from Anne's point of view. Set the other half the task of writing the event from Henry's point of view. Ask the children to share their stories and compare them.

▶ Provide time and materials for the children to draw their own humorous pictures or cartoons of the event. Suggest they label their pictures with the comments made by Anne and Henry using speech bubbles.

Description of Henry VIII

PAGE 32

This description of Henry VIII reflects the very high esteem in which Henry was held in his youth. He was seen as the ideal young man, handsome, fair, well educated, sporting and talented in the arts. It reveals how Henry capitalised on this by dressing in the latest fashions, suggesting also that he may have been quite vain about his appearance. It does show, however, how well educated he was, and was able to speak several languages. His discussion about the King of France reveals his slightly deceitful nature and his interest in politics; while avoiding direct contact with Louis he wants to know all about him and about the events of the war. The final jousting incident confirms Henry's vanity and his desire to show off his expertise as widely as possible to build up his reputation.

Discussing the account

▶ Ask the children when this account was written.
▶ Discuss the meaning of *contemporary* and *firsthand*.
▶ Explain the distinction between primary and secondary sources, explaining that this is a primary source.
▶ Discuss why Henry was so keen to show off. Talk about what this tells us about him.
▶ Ask volunteers to find other examples of Henry's vanity.
▶ Ask individuals to list Henry's achievements.
▶ Ask whether the children think he was a very special person or not.
▶ Discuss whether these qualities will have made him a good king.

Activities

▶ Use the account as part of a shared writing session to make a list of the features that it mentions. Then display the account alongside the portraits of Henry from the CD and ask the children to add other points they have noticed about him from the portraits.

▶ Challenge the children to write a negative description of Henry, pointing out all his worst features and faults. They might enjoy working in pairs on this activity.

▶ Set up a hot-seating situation where a child takes on the role of Henry to answer questions put to him by the class.

Tudor word cards

monarch
court
courtier
Catholic
Protestant
Henry VIII was one of England's most powerful monarchs.
Henry changed England from a Catholic country to a Protestant country.

Government word cards

state
religion
alliance
power
advisers
Henry broke with Rome to gain greater power in England and abroad.
Henry made alliances to gain greater power abroad.

Describing people word cards

proud
timid
fierce
sly
cold
jovial
Catherine of Aragon appears timid and shy in her portrait.
Henry VIII looks arrogant and strong.

Connectives word cards

because
but
and
so
if
Henry divorced Catherine of Aragon because she could not give him a son.
Henry married Anne of Cleves but he did not like her.

Tudor timeline

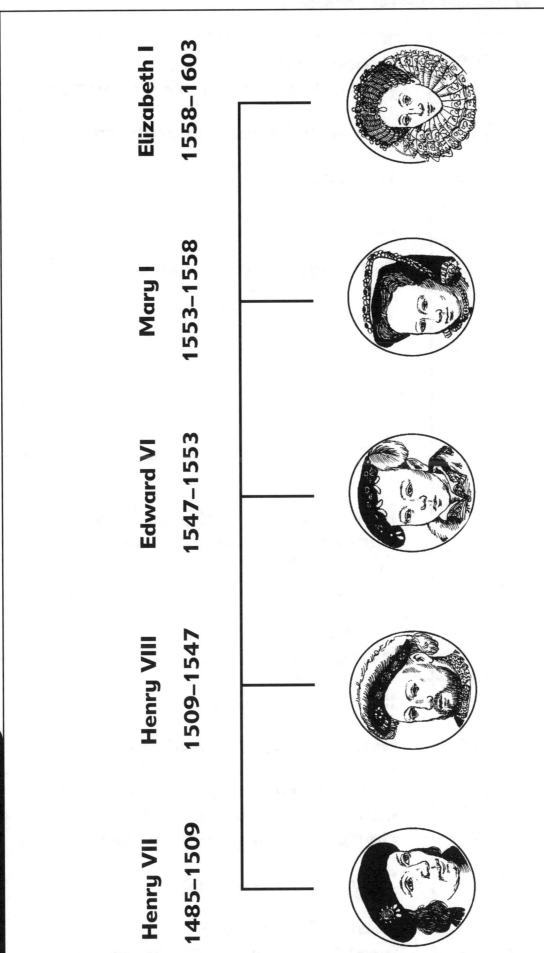

Henry VII	Henry VIII	Edward VI	Mary I	Elizabeth I
1485–1509	1509–1547	1547–1553	1553–1558	1558–1603

Henry VIII timeline

1509	Accession of Henry VIII Henry marries Catherine of Aragon
1512–1514	War with France and Scotland
1516	Mary born
1522	First voyage around the world
1533	Henry divorces Catherine of Aragon Henry marries Anne Boleyn Elizabeth born
1534	Henry sets up Church of England
1536	Anne Boleyn executed Henry marries Jane Seymour
1537	Edward born Jane Seymour dies
1540	Henry marries Anne of Cleves Henry divorces Anne of Cleves Henry marries Catherine Howard
1542	Catherine Howard executed
1543	Henry marries Catherine Parr
1545	Sinking of *Mary Rose*
1547	Death of Henry VIII

Story of Anne of Cleves

nne was the daughter of the Duke of Cleves, a small German kingdom. She had grown up quietly, and had been a very serious child. She worked hard and learned all the things she should know to be a good wife. These included things to do with the running of a home, such as the ordering of food, deciding what meals and menus she would want, managing the servants, and so on. Her father was proud of her, and she was known to all around Europe.

⌘

It was no surprise to Anne and her family when the famous King Henry VIII of England sent his court painter, Hans Holbein to paint her portrait, along with that of her sister to send back for Henry to look at. Anne knew that Henry's wife had only recently died, and that he wanted a new wife. She was very excited at the thought of becoming Queen of England. Everyone was very pleased with the portraits. Hans had made both the sisters look very beautiful, and Anne hoped that Henry would like her picture. Henry, of course, did like the portrait, and as soon as he saw it he asked for her to be sent across the sea to England, to become his wife. Anne was very excited to be going to England to have her very own house to run.

⌘

Journeys in those days took a very long time, and they were also very tiring, jogging along the bumpy roads in cold, dark carriages. So on the way, Anne stayed for the night at a small royal palace. She was taken to her own set of rooms, which she thought quite grand, and began to sort out her things and get ready to go to bed. Meantime, Henry had heard that she was on her way. He had found where she was staying, and thought to himself, "What a joke! I will go ahead to meet her and surprise her with my wit and charm."

⌘

Henry was very proud of his own cleverness, and liked to play practical jokes on everyone. All the courtiers had to pretend they thought this was funny because Henry had a terrible temper, and they did not dare to upset him.

⌘

So Henry hid himself in Anne's chamber, dressed as a court jester. He had borrowed his jester's costume especially for the prank. Suddenly, as Anne was busy tidying her gowns, out leapt Henry from behind the curtains, dressed in the jester's outfit, laughing wildly. Anne was furious. "How dare you, you silly knave," she shouted. "Get out of my room at once, you are a really stupid fellow!" At this, Henry removed the mask he had been wearing to cover his face and went to speak to Anne, but she was even more furious by now, and ordered him to leave at once. Henry stormed out of the room, declaring that if this was his future queen, he did not like her at all. Henry never liked poor Anne, and although they were married, he divorced her six months later and sent her to live far away from the court. Anne did not mind; she was happy to have her own home to run.

Description of Henry VIII

The Venetian ambassador to Henry's court wrote the following description in 1515.

His Majesty is the handsomest king I ever set eyes on; above the usual height, with an extremely fine calf to his leg, his complexion very fair and bright, with auburn hair combed straight and short, in the French fashion, his throat being rather long and thick. He will enter his twenty-fifth year the month after next. He speaks French, English, and Latin, and a little Italian, plays well on the lute and harpsichord, sings from book at sight, draws the bow with greater strength than any man in England, and jousts marvelously. Believe me, he is in every respect a most accomplished Prince; and I, who have now seen all the sovereigns in Christendom, and last of all these two of France and England in such great state, might well rest content.

Later that year, his Majesty came into our arbour, and addressing me in French, said: "Talk with me awhile! The King of France, is he as tall as I am?" I told him there was but little difference. He continued, "Is he as stout?" I said he was not; and he then inquired, "What sort of legs has he?" I replied "Spare." Whereupon he opened the front of his doublet, and placing his hand on his thigh, said "Look here! and I have also a good calf to my leg." He then told me that he was very fond of this King of France, and that for the sake of seeing him, he went over there in person, and that on more than three occasions he was very near him with his army, but that he never would allow himself to be seen, and always retreated, which his Majesty attributed to deference for King Louis, who did not choose an engagement to take place; and he here commenced discussing in detail all the events of that war, and then took his departure.

After dinner, his Majesty and many others armed themselves cap-a-pie, and he chose us to see him joust, running upwards of thirty courses, in one of which he capsized his opponent, who is the finest jouster in the whole kingdom, horse and all. He then took off his helmet, and came under the windows where we were, and talked and laughed with us to our very great honour, and to the surprise of all beholders.

RICH AND POOR IN TUDOR TIMES

Content, skills and concepts

This chapter relates to Unit 8 in the QCA Scheme of Work for history at Key Stage 2. Together with the Rich and poor in Tudor times Resource Gallery on the CD, it introduces a range of visual and written resources that focus on the question 'What were the differences between the lives of rich and poor people in Tudor times?'. These can be used in teaching about the Tudor period, everyday life and the lives of both rich and poor people during that time, as well as some of the discoveries of Tudor artefacts. It also provides materials to support the teaching of key historical concepts relevant to this period and theme.

Children will already have gained experience, while working on other history units, of sequencing and using timelines, using time-related vocabulary, asking and answering questions, and using pictures and written sources. Recounting stories about the past, and looking for similarities and differences between the past and the present are all other prior learning activities which will have introduced relevant skills and concepts to the children in previous years, before they progress to the skills and concepts in this unit. Suggestions for the further development of these skills form part of this chapter.

Resources on the CD-ROM

Pictures of exteriors and interiors of different houses, some built for the rich and others for the poor, as well as illustrations showing aspects of everyday life in Tudor times and photographs of Tudor artefacts are provided on the CD. Teacher's notes containing background information about these resources are provided in this chapter, along with ideas for further work on them.

Photocopiable pages

Photocopiable resources within the book (and also provided in PDF format on the CD from which they can be printed) include:

▶ a timeline
▶ word and sentence cards which highlight the essential vocabulary of this topic
▶ stories and accounts about everyday life.

The teacher's notes that accompany the photocopiable pages include suggestions for developing discussion and using them as whole class, group or individual activities. The accounts and stories about everyday life for the rich and poor have been written at a variety of reading levels and introduce topic-specific vocabulary. The story about the lives of Tudor children will involve and motivate them.

History skills

Skills such as observing, describing, using time-related vocabulary, sequencing, using a timeline, understanding the meaning of dates, comparing, inferring, listening, speaking, reading, writing and drawing are involved in the activities provided. For example, there is an opportunity to develop independent skills in sequencing through the use of the timeline, and to extend their ability to describe and compare the ways of different groups of people in the past.

Historical understanding

In the course of the suggested tasks, a further overarching aim is for children to begin to develop a more detailed knowledge of the past and their ability to sequence and date events independently, through their understanding of the context and content of the factual information they use. They will begin to give reasons for events, use sources to find further information and be able to recount and rewrite the stories and accounts they have heard. They will also have the opportunity to extend their skills in using descriptive language and specific time-related terms in beginning to write their own factual accounts of the past.

NOTES ON THE CD-ROM RESOURCES

Rich person's house

This illustration shows a large, well-furnished Tudor house of the type to have been owned by a rich merchant. It is of the typical Tudor design, with overhanging (or 'jettied') first-floor rooms, tall chimneys and distinctive beams which form the characteristic 'black and white' features of Tudor houses. The beams were, in some parts of the country, painted with back tar to protect them against the weather, and the wattle and daub sections between them were coated with lime for the same purpose. This created the black and white effect. There are several large bedrooms for the family which are comfortably furnished, with carpets, four-poster beds, small tables, chairs or stools and are heated by open fires. A further small, less comfortable servant's bedroom can be seen in the loft space. This room is sparsely furnished and the bed also considerably less comfortable.

On the ground floor is the great hall, entered via large double doors made of solid oak. The main dining table is in this room, set out with typical Tudor tableware, in front of a large open fire. In the kitchen there is another large fireplace, where the cooking of the family meals takes place. The cook can be seen here, stirring food in a large cooking pot over the fire. It is a well-equipped kitchen, with plenty of utensils and implements. A pair of bellows lean against the wall by the fire. Next door there is a small sitting room, where spinning and writing take place. There is a 'settle' there which can seat two or three people. The scullery and outhouses contain the rest of the household and gardening tools needed by the servants, and in the background a large water butt and half-open stable doors are just visible. The corner of a very neat, highly stylised flowerbed can also be seen.

Discussing the illustration

▶ Ask the children what kind of picture this is (a cutaway illustration).
▶ Ask them what kind of person is likely to have owned a house like this, rich or poor. Discuss the reasons for their decision.
▶ Discuss how they know that it is not a modern house, and what features suggest it is from Tudor times, for example the tall chimneys, the wooden beams, the 'black and white' pattern on the front, the spiral staircase, the formal garden.
▶ Discuss the different rooms that are visible. Can the children identify their functions from the furniture inside?
▶ Ask the children to identify objects inside each room that tell us this was a wealthy owner. For example, the four-poster bed, the tableware, and so on.
▶ Talk about how the house was made and how this accounts for the distinctive 'black and white' patterns. Discuss why they were built with 'jettied' upper floors, for example to create more space cheaply.

Activities

▶ Locate the Tudor period on a general class timeline. Talk about why we still see Tudor houses today, and discuss the idea of 'mock' Tudor buildings.
▶ Provide materials for the children to make a simple rectangular box structure, and then a triangular one for the roof. Ask the children to assemble a house made from this frame, and then finish it in the traditional colours.
▶ Ask the children to draw a floor plan for the ground and first floors of this house. Provide them with support for their first attempt, perhaps putting in a number of rooms to show them how to make the plan.
▶ Compare this house with 'Poor person's house' (provided on the CD).

Poor person's house

This is an illustration of a typical home of a poor person in Tudor times. It contrasts strongly with the previous picture. This home appears to have changed little since early medieval times. It is quite small and consists only of one large room. The Tudor people who lived here would have had to cook, work, and sleep in this area, with a bed against the wall and a second bed in part of the roof space. Even the animals lived under one roof, behind a simple partition made of wicker work.

Cooking would have been carried out over a simple fire, the smoke rising through a hole in the roof. Beds were made of straw with a sheet and sometimes a blanket as covers. Everything that the family possessed was kept in this simple house, including the father's working tools, in this case farming tools. Sacks and barrels containing food supplies would also be kept in the room, in this case up in the loft space, where it would have been drier. Apart from cooking arrangements and beds, there would have been little furniture, and here we see some small three-legged stools and a small table.

Discussing the illustration

▶ Identify the type of illustration this is (a cutaway).
▶ Ask the children what type of family would have lived here, rich or poor. Discuss their reasons for making their decision, for example small, one room, one storey, few windows, animals living inside it and so on.
▶ Point out that this would not have been the type of house lived in by the very poorest people in Tudor times; they would have had houses simply made of mud, mixed with straw, with no timber frame or supports.
▶ Discuss where the people slept, ate and rested.
▶ Discuss what the various items in the house are, for example flour barrel, farming tools, cauldron and so on.
▶ Ask the class if they think this would be a comfortable house to live in, and ask them why not, for example smoky, small, little furniture, beds not very soft or warm, cold in winter, and so on.
[NB: remember to discuss issues to do with poverty with sensitivity, especially in relation to unemployment, illness, bereavement, refugees, and so on.]

Activities

▶ Provide materials for the children to make a simple frame for a house on the same pattern as this one, and then complete the exterior.
▶ Show the children how to make simple 'nets' for cuboids, leaving flaps for the roof. Let the children make some nets of their own in stiff paper and assemble them into small cottages, which they can then paint.
▶ Provide the children with a simple writing frame for them to complete about the work that the people shown would have done. Ask them to use the objects in the picture as clues, for example cooking with the sacks of food and barrels; farm work with the tools; looking after animals, such as the pig; mending the tools and house; cleaning, and so on.
▶ Ask the children to draw a simple floor plan of this house.
▶ Compare this house with 'Rich person's house' (provided on the CD).

Stately home: exterior

This photograph of Hardwick Hall shows the imposing façade of this famous stately home. Hardwick, one of the most important stately homes of the Tudor period, was built for Elizabeth, Countess of Shrewsbury, a significant figure in the court of Elizabeth I. Elizabeth, or 'Bess' as she was known, is famous for her responsibility for Mary Queen of Scots.

Completed in 1597, this house is known for its large windows and dominates the surrounding countryside. It stands in a huge park, within which there are gardens of several kinds. Hardwick is still furnished in part, and contains a large collection of Tudor furniture and tapestries. Just visible in the photograph are the initials of Elizabeth, E.S., carved as part of the decorative summits of the two large towers.

Discussing the photograph

▶ Discuss what kind of picture it is, for example a modern photograph.
▶ Ask if they think this is a modern building and ask them to give reasons for their answers.
▶ Tell them about Bess of Hardwick and the date of the building.
▶ Ask the children to point out features of the building that show the Countess of Shrewsbury's wealth, for example the large windows; the size of the building; the huge grounds that it is standing in, and so on.
▶ Discuss why Bess might have wanted such a large house. For example, Bess might have wanted to aspire to the high style of life enjoyed by the landed aristocracy and the royal family, so that she could entertain them appropriately and win their approval.

▶ Consider with the class how many people must have been needed to run such a large house; talk about what servants would have been employed, such as maid, cook, and so on.

▶ Ask whether the children would like to live in a house like this and discuss the reasons 'for' and 'against'.

▶ Talk about why many of these large houses are now looked after by the National Trust or by English Heritage. For example, too big for one person to run; too expensive.

Activities

▶ Use a map of the British Isles to locate Hardwick Hall and help the children to place the date of its building on a timeline of the Tudor period.

▶ Use the photograph to enable the children to make their own paintings and drawings of Hardwick Hall.

▶ Ask the children to imagine what some of the rooms are like. Look at the photograph of 'Stately home: interior' (provided on the CD). Begin some shared descriptive writing about such a room with the whole class, and suggest that they write endings to their descriptions.

▶ Find out further information about Bess of Hardwick. Make this available to the children and ask them to make notes about her.

▶ Suggest that the children look up the names of other Tudor stately homes and make a list of these. They can then locate and mark them on a map of Britain.

▶ Ask the children to find out about the work of servants and masters who lived in these stately homes and to write about their jobs. The children can then give short talks to the rest of the class.

Stately home: interior

This photograph of the dining room in Hardwick Hall indicates the scale and grandeur of the building. From the inside, one is even more aware of the huge leaded window, which gives a very light, airy appearance to the room. The long, heavy table is Persian, made from hardwood, with highly ornate, turned legs. Set with the silver tableware, cutlery and candlesticks, it will have been a most impressive centrepiece for a Tudor banquet.

Other heavy pieces of furniture, including a large sideboard, are ranged around the walls. These are carved in fine detail. The portraits of family members and important acquaintances that adorn the walls are also large and impressive, giving a majestic feel to the house. This, no doubt, was intended as a means of increasing the status and prestige of its owner, Elizabeth, Countess of Shrewsbury.

Discussing the photograph

▶ Ask the class what kind of building this interior shows. Explain to the children that this is the interior of the stately home they looked at above.

▶ Discuss the clues that tell us the type of house it is, for example large windows, high ceiling, large table, expensive portraits, and so on.

▶ Introduce to the children some of the appropriate vocabulary associated with this photograph, for example *leaded windows*, *pewter plate*, *tapestries*, *gilt picture frame*, *wood panelling*.

▶ Look at the style of the furniture and ask the children to think of adjectives to describe it, for example *heavy*, *large*, *dark*, *solid*, *chunky*, and so on.

▶ Discuss what it must have been like when the table was set for a large banquet, and ask the children to suggest things that would have been there, for example expensive gold and silver tableware, servants, expensive foods (swans, fruits), and so on.

▶ Ask if the children will have enjoyed living in a house like this.

Activities

▶ If possible, arrange a visit to a Tudor stately home. Take digital photographs if this is permitted and make sketches of both the exterior and interior and once back in the classroom use them to make a display.

▶ If a visit is not possible, use resources to find out more about the interiors of stately homes. Collect pictures of the different rooms that the children find.

▶ Make a class book about Tudor stately homes, including a list and maps showing the different ones. Send for guidebooks about the houses and use information and pictures from these to build up the class book.

▶ Compare this photograph with the other photographs of Tudor interiors on the CD such as 'Merchant's house: interior' and 'Cottage: interior'.

Merchant's house: exterior

This is a photograph of Paycocke's House, built by a wealthy Tudor woollen merchant in Coggeshall, Essex. It was built around 1500, by John Paycocke as a gift for his son, Thomas. This was a comfortable house, which reflected the owner's wealth and status in society. Houses such as this would have been built either with a timber frame or with stone, depending on the area and the materials that were more readily available. The large windows in this house suggest a wealthy owner, since it was fashionable to show off your wealth by having as much glass as you could afford, glass being very expensive in Tudor times. It is thought that when it was built the house contained rooms for the family to live in, a warehouse for the wool and an office, as well as space for the making of cloth. The upper storeys were built to overhang, since this was a cheap way of increasing the floor area of the rooms.

The house was built using a wooden box frame on stone or rubble foundations. The spaces between the beams of the frame were filled with smaller beams, and the remaining spaces filled with bricks or wattle and daub. Wattles were thin stakes, with finer branches woven between them to form a strong mesh. The wattle mesh would then be coated with clay, mud or plaster mixed with straw, and this was known as daub. In parts of England, the exposed wooden beams would be painted with tar to protect them from the weather, and the wattle and daub would be painted white, also to protect it, producing the traditional 'black and white' houses of the period. Where this was not so necessary, the wood remained a natural colour, as in this picture.

Discussing the photograph
▶ Ask the children to describe the features of the house that indicate its age, for example the roof, the style of the doors and windows, the exposed beams.
▶ Discuss the kind of person who might have owned such a house. Tell the children who did own this house.
▶ Discuss what features suggest that it would have been built for a rich person, for example size of the house, the large windows, the carved beams.
▶ Explain how a house with large windows was very expensive to build.
▶ Look at the large entrance at the far end of the building and encourage the children to work out why there was an entrance like this, for example for horses and carts to enter.
▶ Discuss why the upstairs rooms jutted out, or 'jettied'. Why would the owners want more space? What might the rooms have been used for?

Activities
See 'Merchant's house: interior', below.

Merchant's house: interior

Inside Paycocke's House, the beams are highly decorated and the walls plastered and painted. The room in this picture is large and airy with plenty of light from the large windows. The heavy wooden door is panelled in typical Tudor fashion and there is also a solid wooden floor. The furnishings, including the table, settle, dresser and clock are similarly made of dark, heavy wood. The large central light, although shown here with an electric fitting, would have held large, slow-burning candles. Other candles would have been used to light the room, such as those in the two pewter candlesticks on the table. The warm tapestries and carpets shown on the floor would have been shipped from the Far and Middle East and would have been used to make the home more warm and comfortable.

Discussing the photograph
▶ Ask the children what part of the house this picture shows.
▶ Discuss the features that indicate that it is the house of a wealthy person, for example the furniture, the windows, the carpet, and so on.
▶ Ask for volunteers to provide words to describe the style of the interior furnishings that characterise the period, for example, rich carpets, detailed, decorative windows, heavy wooden furniture, and so on.

▶ Discuss the materials used to make the objects seen in this interior.
▶ Talk about where some of the items might have been made, for example the carpet.
▶ Ask the children if they would have liked to live in a house like this. Discuss what it would have been like at night, and ask the children to describe their own ideas.

Activities
▶ Locate this house on a map of Britain and on a class timeline.
▶ Ask the children to find out why merchants became rich during the Tudor period. In particular, why did merchants selling wool and woollen goods become so rich?
▶ Provide painting and colouring materials in different media for the children to make their own pictures of typical rich Tudor houses, both interiors and exteriors.

Cottage: exterior

This is a photograph of a typical 'cruck cottage', a common type of small Tudor house. They were known as 'cruck cottages' because the cruck, or arch formed by the trunk of a tree and a strong, outgrowing branch, would be used to make the basic frame for the building. Two inverted Vs, formed by the trees would be placed at each end of the house and the roof created by joining them with a beam to form a ridge. This style of cottage was the cheapest type to build. However, many people could not afford timber-framed buildings at all, and their homes were made of 'cob', a mixture of mud, lime and straw, painted white, yellow or pink, and with thatched roofs.

This cruck cottage has smaller beams with a steeply sloping thatched roof and at one time would have had wattle and daub walls. Here we can see the traditional patterns created by the thatcher on finishing off and securing the thatch along the ridges of the roof. The second-floor rooms were built into the roof space, and so these would have been quite small, with sloping ceilings inside. This cottage has modernised windows, with large panes of glass. The original windows would have been smaller since glass was very expensive.

Discussing the photograph
▶ Explain the type of house this is (a 'cruck' cottage).
▶ Talk about the size of the cottage, for example could it be very large, given the way the frame was made?
▶ Discuss whether it would have been the home of a rich person.
▶ Look at the distinctive features of the cottage and ask the children to point out those which tell us it is from the Tudor period.
▶ Explain how cottages in some parts of the country came to be the typical 'black and white' colour.
▶ Discuss what it would have been like to live in a house like this.
▶ Ask the children to point out any features they can see that look more modern than the cottage itself, for example the glass panes in the windows; the chimneys. Why do they think this has happened?

Activities
See 'Cottage: interior', below.

Cottage: interior

This is a photograph of the interior of what is known as the cottage of Anne Hathaway. It is called a cottage now but in fact in Tudor times it was a farmhouse. Although far from being the home of a really poor person in Tudor times, it does show some of the features of a less affluent house. The beams are roughly carved and left unadorned. The floors are of stone, and the leaded windows are quite small. There is a very large stone fireplace, supported by a huge wooden lintel. The walls are partly lined with wooden panels and the furniture is made from dark, heavy wood as in the other homes above. In general, there is much less ornamentation and luxurious soft furnishing than in the homes of the richer people. The stone floors are bare and there is also less light. Homes such as these would have been lit by fewer, smaller candles, which would have been moved around the house as required. This house, however, would have been fairly comfortable, compared with the small cottages and huts of the very poor, who would have had little other than a fire, a stool and a bed made of straw.

Discussing the photograph

▶ Look at the photograph and ask for volunteers to point out the details that tell us this is part of a Tudor home, for example the beams, the wooden panelling, the large fireplace, the tableware above the fireplace, and so on.

▶ Tell the children who lived in this house.

▶ Discuss whether the owner of this house was rich or poor. Explain that they were probably not very rich, nor very poor.

▶ Explain to the class how a very poor cottage would have been made, and how little there would have been inside it.

Activities

▶ Compare the different types of homes 'Stately home', 'Merchant's house', 'Cottage' and the 'Poor person's house' (provided on the CD) and discuss how they came to be built in such different ways, for example because of the money available to the owners. Compare the exteriors and the interiors, and discuss the differences. In comparing all three interiors, point out how each home still contained fairly similar heavy wooden furniture. Ask the children to try to work out why everyone except the extremely poor could afford such good wooden furniture, for example, wood was plentiful and cheap.

▶ Ask the children to try to imagine how different it would be to have lived in a small cottage like this, compared with Hardwick Hall (see 'Stately home: exterior' and 'Stately home: interior' on the CD). Ask them which they think they might have preferred and why.

▶ Compare 'Cottage: interior' with 'Merchant's house: interior' (provided on the CD). Ask for volunteers to point out the subtle differences between the two, for example the smaller windows, the lack of carpets, the plain beams without carving, and so on.

▶ Give the children a grid to complete outlining the similarities and differences between these Tudor houses and houses in the present day. The children could work on these in pairs and discuss their ideas.

▶ Make two display boards, one labelled, 'Rich Tudor homes' and the other 'Poor Tudor homes'. Ask the children to select and organise the information they have found and display it to contrast the two ways of life.

Rich merchant and wife

This is a modern illustration of what a wealthy merchant would have looked like. During the Tudor period merchants began to travel further afield, and trade increased for wool merchants especially, who were able to import luxury goods in large quantities. This merchant is well dressed, with his hair neatly trimmed along with a smart beard, which was fashionable at the time. He wears leather shoes, doublet and hose, tunic and ruff and a smart hat with a feather. His long coat is trimmed with fur to show to the world his affluence. In addition, his sleeves are fashionably 'slashed' in the style favoured by Henry VIII. To further show his wealth, he carries a bag of gold.

The merchant's wife is also dressed in the style of costume in favour at court. She wears a neat headdress, a large ruff and the wide dress and puffed sleeves which were fashionable at that time. Her sleeves are elaborately detailed and her dress, which would have been of very fine material such as silk, velvet or brocade, is patterned with most intricate embroidery. She will also have worn smart leather shoes, which usually had elegant heels. The merchant and his wife will have taken care to dress smartly to reveal both their success and to further their social ambitions.

Discussing the illustration

▶ Tell the children that this is an illustration of a rich merchant and his wife. Explain who merchants were and how they became rich in Tudor times.

▶ Ask the children to think of adjectives to describe the appearance of the man and woman in this illustration.

▶ Ask the children to explain why they might have chosen such expensive materials as fur and silk for their clothes.

▶ Ask if they are trying to copy someone else, as happens in changing fashions today, for example the people at court, the nobility. Discuss why they would want to do this.

▶ Talk about the practicality of their clothes, for example would they have been able to work very easily while wearing them?

▶ Discuss the names of the different items of their costumes and introduce some of the archaic terms used to describe them, for example *hose, doublet, jerkin, chemise, ruff*.

▶ Show the children the photographs 'Merchant house: exterior' and 'Merchant house: interior' (provided on the CD) and explain that this couple would have lived in a house like to that one

Activities

▶ Discuss how it is that we know about these people from so long ago. In a shared writing session, write a brief piece about the sources that we can use to find out about such people, for example portraits, woodcuts, written descriptions.

▶ Draw round two children on large pieces of paper and then use these outlines to make collages in fabrics and other materials of a rich man and woman. Try to provide rich-looking fabrics to resemble silk, satin and velvet.

▶ Look at the two photographs of 'Merchant's house: exterior' and 'Merchant's house: interior' (provided on the CD). Ask the children to find out other details about a merchant's life.

▶ Compare this couple with the illustrations of the 'Poor man and woman' (provided on the CD, also see below).

Poor man and woman

Most ordinary poor people would have worked in some capacity on the land in Tudor times. This illustration shows a farmhand who will have been at the lowest end of the social scale. As with all Tudor people, he wears a hat and is simply, but warmly dressed. Like the merchant, he wears a beard, which was the current fashion, although it will not have been as smartly trimmed. He wears strong shoes and gaiters over his trousers. These were worn to keep long clothes dry and out of the mud, and will have been tied closely round the legs to avoid the trousers becoming soaked by long, wet grass. The clothes of poor people will have been fastened with rough thread or twine, rather than buttons or hooks. As can be seen, his belt was an important part of his dress, since he was able to use it to keep his tools in.

The woman wears a simple scarf around her head, to keep her hair from her face while she was working. She may also have worked at jobs on the land, helping to gather the harvests, winnowing (separating the wheat from the chaff by throwing the grain in the air) and milking. Her clothes were therefore simple compared with those of court ladies or rich merchants' wives. She will have worn a long skirt, made of rough woollen material, a blouse with a bodice over the top, and a large apron to keep her clothes as clean as possible. She will have worn simple, flat leather shoes and may also have used a belt to store articles for her work.

Discussing the illustration

▶ Ask the class to describe the type of clothing worn by the people in this illustration. Point out, however, that these are working people, rather than the extremely poor.

▶ Ask the children to point to the objects or items of clothing that tell us something about the people wearing them, for example the tools of their trade.

▶ Discuss why poor people dressed like this, for example to be ready for their work, practical for working in.

▶ Compare the clothes of working people in Tudor times with those of working people today, and ask what is different about them.

▶ Ask if working people today have to wear their working clothes all the time and discuss the reasons why not.

▶ Point out the old-fashioned items of clothing they can see in each picture, such as gaiters, jerkin, bodice, and so on.

▶ Discuss the kinds of fabric used in the clothes of the poor, and what it is likely to have been like, for example rough materials, plain colours. Ask the children to give reasons for their suggestions, for example the material will have been strong and tough because they did not want it to wear out.

▶ Talk about the colours of the clothes worn by the poor, for example dull because dyes were expensive.

Activities

▶ Draw around two children on large pieces of paper and then use these outlines to make collages in rough, dull-coloured materials of a poor man and woman. Display these next to the collages of the rich (see above).

▶ Devise a short role-play activity where the children re-enact some of the jobs they have seen the poor portrayed as doing.
▶ Carry out a hot-seating activity, where you dress up as a poor person and the children interview you about what you like and dislike about your life.
▶ Compare with the illustrations of the 'Rich merchant and wife' (provided on this CD).

Rich children

Tudor children were dressed in very similar clothes to those of their parents. The little girl in this illustration wears the same neat headdress as her mother might have done, over very carefully tended hair. She wears soft shoes and a long, richly embroidered or patterned dress. Her bodice may have been made of silk, worn over a blouse of fine fabric, finished with lace collar and cuffs. As can be seen here, the children of rich people in Tudor times were provided both with toys and with time to play, unlike the children of the poor, who were expected to work.

The rich boy is also dressed in similar apparel to that of his adult counterparts. He has leather shoes and colourful hose, over which he wears an elegant outfit probably made of velvet or silk. His shirt is elegantly finished with a lace-trimmed collar, and like his parent, he wears a smart hat with a feather, much as we see in the portraits of Henry VIII and Edward VI. Again, like his adult male counterparts, he carries, as part of his costume, a sword and sheath.

Discussing the illustration
▶ Ask the children what they particularly notice or find interesting about the children in the picture, for example they look exactly like the adults at that time. Explain how Tudor children were expected to grow up very rapidly, and to look and behave like their parents.
▶ Tell the children how children usually had to work in Tudor times, and ask them if they think these children would have had to work. Why not?
▶ Discuss what the children think they might have done all day, for example the little girl may have played with her doll, the boy might have learned to be a swordsman.
▶ Talk about the clothes themselves, for example do they look comfortable to wear? Do they look heavy or tight?
▶ Discuss whether the children would have liked to dress like this. Would it have been difficult for them to play?

Activities
See 'Poor children', below.

Poor children

Tudor children from poor backgrounds were poorly dressed. Perhaps the most startling feature of their costume is the lack of shoes. The girl wears a rough dress, underblouse and pinafore, along with a functional cap to cover her hair. Rather than being carefully fashioned, her hair is simply tied back to keep it off her face while working. The girl in this illustration will probably have worked as a housemaid or scullery maid, and will have had to do the most menial and unpleasant tasks around the house, such as cleaning the floors and the cooking pots.

The boy shown here also wears no shoes and only has short trousers. He has a shirt and roughly made jacket which fastens with simple ties. He wears no hat. Many boys in Tudor times worked and this one appears to have had the task of lighting the way for gentlefolk with a burning torch, a dangerous job for such a young child. Both of these poor children may well have had to provide for themselves from what little they earned, or they will have had to take their earnings back to help support others in their families.

Discussing the illustration
▶ Ask whether these children look rich or poor. Do they look like they had to work? What work do they think the children in these pictures had to do? How can they tell?
▶ Ask for individuals to describe the clothes of the boy and girl and to explain what kind of fabrics they are likely to have been made from. For example, cheap, rough and hard wearing. Ask other children to explain why they think this is.
▶ Ask for a volunteer to stand up and get the rest of the class to compare their modern clothes with those in the pictures.

▶ Point out the names of some of the garments which are unfamiliar today, such as *cap*, *breeches*, *pinafore*, and so on.
▶ Talk about the fact that these children have no shoes. Ask the children to think of reasons for this.
▶ Discuss what it must have been like in the winter for these children.

Activities
▶ Compare the illustrations 'Rich children' and 'Poor children' and ask the children to make a note of the main differences they can identify between them.
▶ Set the children the task of writing a piece of extended writing about the lives of rich and poor children, based on the preceding discussions. Give them some of the words that have been introduced and the word cards (see photocopiable pages 53 and 54) to assist them in their writing.
▶ Get the children to act out short dramatic scenes from the daily lives of rich and poor Tudor children.
▶ Tell the class the story of Dick Whittington, who rose from poverty to become Lord Mayor of London and a rich merchant.
▶ Share with the class the stories about everyday life and the contemporary accounts on photocopiable pages 56, 57 and 58.
▶ Ask the children to write letters from rich or poor Tudor children who are writing to their mothers about their lives, or alternatively to keep a regular diary written from this point of view. Use the other illustrations from the CD to provide further information to inform their writing, such as 'Tudor street scene' or 'Crowd playing football'.

Tudor street scene

This illustration shows a busy street scene in a Tudor town. The street itself is narrow and the houses very close together, especially the upper floors which were built out over the road. Everyday life is in full swing, with a housemaid throwing waste water from an upper storey, stallholders and traders selling their wares, such as fresh vegetables, eggs and fish, and people waiting at the pump to fill up their water buckets. The food containers will be of interest to the children, since they are all handmade, such as the wicker baskets of eggs and the wooden barrels used to store drinks and fruit.

It was quite common for all rubbish and most waste water to be thrown into the street, hence the drainage channel often seen running down the centre of old cobbled streets. Much waste would also pile up in the street and the rats would be visible. Farm animals and birds would also wander in the streets. It is easy to see how theft could easily be carried out in these narrow, congested streets, as well as how disease could spread so easily and rapidly through the population. There is a brief glimpse of a rich person on a horse in the background, either a nobleman or a rich merchant. He provides a sharp contrast with the other ordinary people in the street, with his air of authority, dress and smart horse.

Discussing the illustration
▶ Ask the children what kind of picture this is, for example a modern illustration of a scene from many years ago.
▶ Discuss what is happening in the illustration. Ask individuals to find something different to describe.
▶ Suggest that they look for rich people in the illustration. How many can they see? Can they describe them?
▶ Ask if there is anything that surprises them about the illustration, for example the dirty street, things being thrown from the windows.
▶ Get volunteers to describe the things they find rather unpleasant in the illustration.
▶ Discuss why the Tudors kept their streets like this. For example, they did not know very much about hygiene and disease; many had lived in the countryside and did not adapt their way of life to the towns.
▶ Explain that many illnesses could be caught from these conditions, for example rats carried dirt and disease.
▶ Ask the children to look at how close the houses are to one another in the street and notice the narrowness of the street. Point out how this would have made streets congested and dirty.

▶ Point out the rubbish and waste water running down the middle of the street.
▶ Ask if children have ever seen any old cobbled streets like the one shown here.

Activities

▶ If possible, arrange a visit to an old street for the children to look at the way it was made and at the cobbles.
▶ Create a 3-D collage with models of houses projecting from the wall. Provide many different textures and materials for the children to use to reconstruct the picture on the wall. Ask them to write descriptive pieces to accompany the display.
▶ Tell the children about street sellers and the street cries they may have used (flower sellers, fruit and vegetable sellers, and so on). Challenge the children to make up some street cries of their own.
▶ Write a diary extract from the point of view of the rich man riding through the street, describing his disgust at the ways of the common people.
▶ Talk about how easy it was for thieves to snatch things in these crowded conditions, and explain to the class about the 'hue and cry', a large crowd that would form to chase a thief who had been noticed through the streets, adding to the congestion. Also refer the children to the illustration 'Crowd playing football' (provided on the CD).

Crowd playing football

Football is a game dating back many hundreds of years. It is said to have originated in England, however, where a leather football from Viking times has been discovered. In Tudor England, football would often be played in the streets. In those days, the game appeared to have few if any rules, and anyone who wanted to could join in. This, of course, led to huge crowds sometimes forming. Fights and disorder would break out as the crowd rushed and jostled for the ball. The football itself can be seen here as a rough leather ball, stitched along the seams to keep it all together. It will have been a solid ball, and would have caused considerable damage to property and injury to anyone hit by it. There was no organised police force in those days to keep order in the streets, which could be quite dangerous places.

Discussing the illustration

▶ Ask the children what game is being played here.
▶ Explain how football is a very old game, and that it was a popular game in Tudor times.
▶ Ask them if they think it is the same sort of game as we play and see today.
▶ Find out what the children think it would have been like in the street when a game like this was going on.
▶ Ask if there was anyone to control it or stop the game if it became too rough.
▶ Look at the bystanders and discuss whether they look as if they are enjoying watching the game or not.

Activities

▶ Find out further information about the game of football in Tudor times. See if the children can find information about the game being played at other times in history, and help the children to place these pieces of information on the class timeline.
▶ Ask the children to work in pairs or small groups to write a detailed list of the rules in present-day football, and then compare this with the Tudor version of the game.
▶ Set the children the task of finding out about the other games that were played by both children and adults in Tudor times. They can then talk to the rest of the class about their findings.

Lute

This lute is one of a family of stringed instruments which were played by plucking the strings with the fingers. This example is a very simple type likely to have been owned by a middle-class person. Some lutes of the later Tudor period owned by richer people were finely designed and decorated. The number of strings on a lute could vary, and the larger the lute, the more elaborate it would have been and the greater the number of strings and notes it could play. The lute was, along with the recorder, one of the most popular musical instruments of the time, and it was played to accompany religious readings and songs and was known to have been played by Henry VIII himself. Music was a pastime for the rich and it was also popular with the monarchy in Tudor times.

Discussing the artefact

▶ Discuss what kind of picture this is, for example a modern photograph of a Tudor lute.
▶ Ask the children what this would have been used for and how they think it was probably played.
▶ Explain how this was one of the most popular instruments in Tudor times, and how most wealthy and fairly well-off families would own one.
▶ Discuss whether this particular type of lute would have belonged to a rich or a less well-off family, and get the children to give their reasons for their decisions. For example, it belonged to a less well-off family as it is quite plain.
▶ Discuss what the lute is likely to have sounded like, and whether it was a soft or loud instrument.

Activities

▶ Play some pieces of lute music to the class, such as 'Greensleeves' (provided in the Henry VIII Resource Gallery on the CD).
▶ Give the children drawing materials for making observational drawings of the lute.
▶ Provide the children with a variety of sources, such as information books and access to the Internet, to research other kinds of musical instruments that were played in Tudor times.
▶ If possible, bring in to the class a real lute for the children to see and touch.

Baby's cradle

Many of the items made for babies and small children in Tudor times, such as cradles, rattles and even baby walkers, bear a surprising resemblance to their modern-day equivalents. This wooden cradle is beautifully made and, although it is not complete, it has some interesting features. It has been designed so that it rests in a frame from which it is suspended in such a way that it will swing from side to side very easily. The wooden supports for the frame are carefully carved as birds which look down on the baby in the cradle, perhaps as an early type of cot toy. The slots were designed for ties or straps to be fastened to prevent the baby falling out when the cradle was rocked.

Discussing the artefact

▶ Ask the children what they think this object is.
▶ Discuss what kind of family might have used it.
▶ Talk about what it is made from.
▶ Discuss how it worked and how it could have been rocked by the foot.
▶ Talk about who might have rocked the baby, for example a servant.
▶ Look at the details on the cradle, for example the birds and the slots near the top.
▶ Discuss what the uses of these features might have been.
▶ Explain that it was common for babies to be tied into their cots for safety.
▶ Tell the children about swaddling – the tight bandaging that was wrapped around small babies to prevent them from moving. It was thought that they would grow straight and fit if they were kept tied up like this.

Activities

▶ Provide art materials for the children to make observational drawings or models of the cradle.
▶ Encourage the children to find further information about the lives of babies and small children in Tudor times, for example what toys did they have, what did they eat, what did they wear and so on. Talk to the class about their findings.
▶ Take the hot seat in the role of 'nurse' to a rich family, and answer children's questions about your work.

Globe of the world

The Tudor age was one of exploration and discovery. Careful maps and charts were made, and affluent people were able to study their own globes of the world. The globes, covered with paper maps of the world, were quite large, and stood on the floor in a metal stand. The globe itself would rotate inside the stand so that any part of the world could be examined with ease. The knowledge, skill and technology involved in producing an item such as this is surprising for such an early period, and the possession of such an item was a significant feature of the homes of the monarchy and the wealthy in the rest of society.

Discussing the artefact
▶ Ask the children what they think this is a photograph of.
▶ Ask how they know that it is quite an old globe of the world.
▶ Discuss how it would have been used.
▶ Discuss how it was that the Tudors could make globes like these.
▶ Discuss who is likely to have had a globe like this in their home in Tudor times.
▶ Talk about whether it would have been easy or cheap to make.
▶ Ask if anyone has a globe like this themselves, and ask them to describe it.
▶ Ask if the children think that all the places we now know of would have been on the globes made in Tudor times. Discuss which parts of the world were not known about, for example Australia.
▶ Ask the children why they think the rich would have wanted an object like this in their homes.

Activities
▶ Compare this globe with a modern one, and ask the children to note each of the differences that they can find. Get them to make a chart showing the most important differences and gradually working down to the less significant differences.
▶ Find out about early maps and globes, and about how they were made.
▶ Tell the children about the very early maps, such as the 'Mappa Mundi', made in medieval times, and Ptolemy's Map which was used by Christopher Columbus.
▶ Challenge them to write an adventure story set in Tudor times, involving a globe of the world and a sea adventure.

Leather-bound book

The Tudor age saw the beginnings of printing and book-making on a large scale. With the introduction of the printing press in about 1450, the production of books, in particular the Bible and Prayer Book, rapidly began to increase. This early book dates from 1552. It is bound in leather and the pages would have been made of fine parchment or paper. Although the invention and proliferation of printing had made books far more accessible and easy to produce than ever before, books such as these remained very labour-intensive to produce. They were hand-bound and the covers would also have had to be gilded and embossed by hand. Consequently, books tended to be extremely expensive, so much so that early Bibles were chained to the pulpits in churches. Privately owned books could only have been purchased by the wealthy.

Discussing the artefact
▶ Discuss what the children can see in this modern photograph. Ask them if they know what the cover would have been made from, for example leather.
▶ Discuss the pages of the book, and explain how when printing became common, the pages in books were no longer made from vellum, as in the days when monks wrote them out by hand, but were made from paper. This was easier to use in a printing machine.
▶ Ask the children to look closely at the numbers on the front of the book, and ask what they think the date is. This was the date that the book was made.
▶ Look closely at the patterned cover, and ask the children to describe what it must have been like when it was new, for example the colours would have been bright, and the lettering would have been in gold.
▶ Look further at the patterns on the cover, and discuss how they may have been 'embossed', or pressed into the leather to make a raised design, which was then painted. Talk about how long this would have taken and how it would have been done, for example by hand.
▶ Ask the children whether this kind of book would have been owned by a rich or poor person. Explain how most early books would have been made for the churches, since they were Bibles and Prayer Books.

Activities
▶ Find copies of old leather-bound books with ornately decorated covers and allow time for the children to look at them and examine how they were made.
▶ Provide drawing materials for the children to copy some of the cover designs.
▶ Provide a variety of book-making materials for the children to learn how to bind their own books. First arrange for the children to design and make the cover. They can then make the spine and stitch in the pages. (They may need adult help at these different stages if they have not made books before.)
▶ The children could use their books in which to keep their best pieces of work in history.
▶ Set the children the task of finding out about the early history of printing, using books and the Internet.
▶ Provide simple printing materials such as sets of letters and printing inks, and let the children make up their own printed pages.

Lady's bodice

This type of rich lady's bodice would have been made of expensive materials, such as silk or satin. The bodice was worn over the top of the chemise, or shirt, a common garment to both men and women. The bodice, however, was specially tailored to emphasise the wearer's slimness at the waist, an especially important feature of Tudor fashion. The design of this example particularly emphasises this feature, along with the low, scooped neckline, which would have revealed the richly embroidered or lace chemise beneath, and allowed room for the deep, starched ruff which was also fashionable at the time. The sleeves are turned back, again to reveal the fine detail in the embroidered, lace-trimmed cuffs.

Man's tunic

Men and boys wore the same items of clothing, and over the shirt or chemise they would wear a tunic like this, otherwise known as a jerkin. Many were made of leather and some would be of silk or satin. They were highly detailed and ornate, again designed to emphasis the slim proportions of the wearer. The high collar would fit beneath the ruff and the short sleeves allowed the richly embroidered sleeves of an undergarment to show. Fine patterns were produced in leather jerkins by punching patterns of small holes to form intricate designs, like that shown here. Fine craftsmanship is also evident in the buttonholes and the small, finely covered buttons. This would have been a very highly prized garment and only available to the very rich.

Discussing the garments
▶ Tell the children the names of these Tudor garments.
▶ Talk about the materials they are made from and discuss how they would have been expensive.
▶ Ask the children what type of people would have worn clothes like these.
▶ Discuss the way they would have been fastened, for example with hooks or tiny buttons, which would have been very expensive to sew on.
▶ Look at the style of the garments, and ask the children what sort of impression the wearers wanted to create, for example to look very slim.
▶ Discuss how these garments would have been worn.

Activities
▶ Look at other illustrations on the CD which show Tudor people's dress, focussing especially on the costumes of the wealthy. Identify these items of clothing, and note the different types of fabric that they could be made from.
▶ Try to collect examples of different materials, such as silk, satin, velvet, soft leather, and bring these for the class to look at and touch.
▶ Get the children to think of descriptive words to describe the different materials you have been discussing, and then ask them to compose short advertisements for garments made from them.
▶ Give the children materials to make small 'catalogues', illustrating all the different Tudor clothes, for men, women and children. They can collect pictures and draw some of their own, and will need to write short descriptions of each item.

▶ Ask the children to look at images of some very famous Tudors, such as Elizabeth I (see 'Queen Elizabeth I' in the Henry VIII Resource Gallery on the CD) and to find the Tudor names for her clothes and then to describe them.

Beggars and sturdy knaves

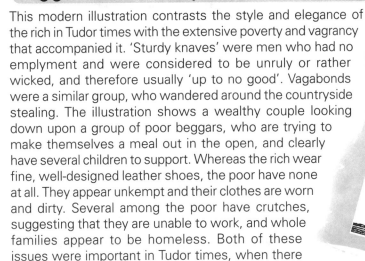

This modern illustration contrasts the style and elegance of the rich in Tudor times with the extensive poverty and vagrancy that accompanied it. 'Sturdy knaves' were men who had no emplyment and were considered to be unruly or rather wicked, and therefore usually 'up to no good'. Vagabonds were a similar group, who wandered around the countryside stealing. The illustration shows a wealthy couple looking down upon a group of poor beggars, who are trying to make themselves a meal out in the open, and clearly have several children to support. Whereas the rich wear fine, well-designed leather shoes, the poor have none at all. They appear unkempt and their clothes are worn and dirty. Several among the poor have crutches, suggesting that they are unable to work, and whole families appear to be homeless. Both of these issues were important in Tudor times, when there was a considerable amount of unemployment and homelessness, due to rapid inflation and landowners' desires to turn more of their property over to sheep farming, where large profits could be made very rapidly. Generally, the rich looked down upon and despised the poor, since it was a common view at the time that the poor deserved their fate – their condition being entirely their own doing.

Discussing the illustration
▶ Ask the children what they think is happening in this illustration.
▶ Point out to the children which are the rich and which are the poor people in the illustration. How do they know?
▶ Think about the reasons for so many people being in the street begging. Ask the children to think of as many reasons as they can, for example the people have no work; they are ill; they have no homes, and so on.
▶ Think about the title of the picture. Why are they called *sturdy knaves*? Explain this term to the children.
▶ Discuss whether the class think the rich people will help the sturdy knaves or not.

Activities
▶ Ask the children to write a definition first in a sentence, then in three or four words, of *sturdy knaves*. Look up different dictionary definitions.
▶ Organise one third of the class to make a 'freeze frame' of the scene shown here. Then organise the other two groups, one to make a freeze frame showing what may have been happening just before this scene and just after it.
▶ Tell the children about how pictures at that time were made, for example usually using 'woodcuts', a cheaper way of reproducing pictures than making paintings and portraits. Show the children how to make their own woodcuts, perhaps using polystyrene tiles instead of wood, and then let them experiment with printing their pictures.

Page from a will

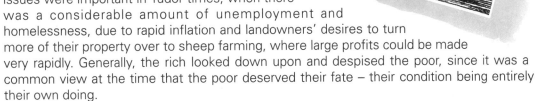

In Tudor times, it became more common for important events in the lives of ordinary people to be recorded. For example, a law was passed that ordered parish priests to record in the parish registers, all the births, marriages and deaths of their parishioners. Similarly, the writing of wills became more common, and should someone die without leaving a will, then a list of their possessions would be drawn up; these were called inventories. Many of these wills and inventories remain and provide us with vast amounts of information about the lives of ordinary people. This example is a corner of a page from a will. The photograph shows the style of handwriting used at the time, with its ornate, stylised initial letter to decorate the page. This style is a remnant of the exquisitely detailed 'illuminated manuscripts' of the Middle Ages, which were now being superseded by the printed word. Children will appreciate the beautiful style of the lettering and will be able to identify occasional words in the text.

Discussing the photograph

▶ Ask the children what kind of picture this is, for example a photograph of some Tudor writing.

▶ Explain how it is just a corner of a page, so that we can see the way the writing was done more clearly.

▶ Ask the children what they think of it, for example does it look very neat? Is it like their writing?

▶ See if the children can identify any words and ask them to point them out.

▶ Look carefully at the initial letter and discuss the style and patterning used to make it.

▶ Discuss the size of the lettering, noting how the first line is made larger. Discuss why this was, for example perhaps it was the most important line, and the writer wanted to be sure the reader looked at this.

▶ Explain that this is a line from a register of wills, and explain why people wrote wills.

Activities

▶ Suggest the children write their own 'wills', or make inventories of what they have in their own bedrooms. Compare these with a Tudor example, noting the different things that we now have.

▶ Give the children some calligraphy materials and ask them to practise their handwriting using these. Suggest they try to produce some decorated lettering with the calligraphy pens. Use different inks to produce coloured letters.

▶ Make a display of the original pieces of writing that have been found and the children's own calligraphy work. Ask the children to make labels and captions for the display.

Wooden plate

This large wooden plate or 'charger' would have been used by poor people, while the rich would have used the same kind of items, but made of pewter, silver, or even gold. Wooden utensils were very common in Tudor times, and people would use wooden spoons, bowls and cups, as well as wooden beer tankards. The charger would have been used to serve a large quantity of the same food for several people. Instead of having individual plates, it was the custom for one large dish to be served and for everyone to help themselves from this, putting their food onto a piece of bread or a wooden trencher. Although very plain, this charger carries much information about its age and possible usage. It may, for example, have been used for a more liquid food, since it is deeper in the hollow than many Tudor plates.

Discussing the artefact

▶ Ask the children what they think the object is in this picture, and what it was used for.

▶ Discuss what it was made from.

▶ Talk about and explain how the rich would have had similar objects as this plate, but they would have been made of materials other than wood, such as pewter, and silver or gold, if they were very rich.

▶ Ask the class why they think wood was used as the material for this plate, for example it was plentiful and therefore cheap.

▶ Tell the children how in Tudor times, forks were not used. People ate with just a knife and their fingers.

Activities

▶ If possible, show the children a modern wooden plate and ask them to look at how it was made, and the skills used in carving or 'turning' the wood.

▶ Look at other items of tableware used in Tudor times – see 'Tableware found on the *Mary Rose*' provided on the CD in the section on Henry VIII.

▶ Set the children the task of making menus for Tudor banquets, which would have been attended by the rich. Then ask them to research and make a list of what a poor person might eat in a day.

Cooking pot

This type of iron cooking pot would have been widely used in kitchens in Tudor England. Designed to contain food for a large number of people, it was used over an open fire. It would have been suspended over the fire, in the same way as the kettles, and lifted using the two handles. Pottage – a kind of stew made with grain, vegetables, and meat if it was available – was the staple diet of the Tudor poor and would have been cooked in a pot such as this one. Salt was expensive and only the rich could afford it. Boiling food in these cauldrons was the commonest form of cooking in the period, along with the spit roasting method, which also took place over an open fire. The fireplaces were always large in wealthy Tudor houses and in cottages, to accommodate the work that was carried out around them.

Discussing the artefact
▶ Discuss what is shown in this photograph.
▶ Ask the children what the cauldron might have been used for.
▶ Explain to the class about pottage.
▶ Explain how the pot would have been regularly used so that pottage was always available.
▶ Ask the children how they think it was heated. Other pots and kettles would also have been hung over the fire like this. Explain that in richer kitchens there might have been an oven for making bread.
▶ Ask the children if they think they would like to eat pottage.

Activities
▶ Find out about the kind of cooking that was done in Tudor times and the types of utensils that were used, such as roasting spits. Divide the class into groups, with half of them looking at the food of the poor and the other half looking at the food of the rich, such as the Court. The children can then present their findings to the other half of the class.
▶ Ask the children to write their own recipes for pottage and porridge.
▶ Bring into the class a collection of different herbs for the children to touch and smell, and explain how herbs were used very widely in Tudor cooking. Explain how they were also used to make medicines and remedies. Let the children experiment with mortars and pestles to mix herbs and make new scents and flavourings. They could put these into little fabric bags to make the room smell good. Lavender is especially useful for this activity, and the children might enjoy making lavender bags to take home.
▶ Read the extract from Shakespeare's *Hamlet*, where Ophelia lists many of the herbs that were used at the time (Act VI Scene V).

NOTES ON THE PHOTOCOPIABLE PAGES

Word and sentence cards

PAGES 53 AND 54

Specific types of vocabulary have been introduced on the word and sentence cards. These words relate to Tudor houses and Tudor society. Encourage the children to think of other appropriate words to add to those provided, in order to build up a word bank for the theme of Rich and poor in Tudor times. They could include words encountered in their research, such as words to do with occupations, homes and clothes. They could also use the cards in labelling displays and in writing simple and complex sentences to record what they have learned. They should also use the word cards as support in descriptive, factual and creative work and in writing discussions and arguments.

Activities
▶ Once you have made copies of the word and sentence cards, cut them out and laminate them, use them as often as possible when talking about the Tudors. They could be used for word and spelling games, or to help less able readers make up their own sentences or phrases.
▶ Add further vocabulary to the set of words, using those suggested by the children.
▶ Make displays of aspects of Tudor life and use word and sentence cards to label and describe them.

▶ Encourage the children to read the labels and sentences to yourself, adult helpers and visitors to the classroom.

▶ Encourage the children to use the words in stories and non-fiction writing as often as possible.

▶ Organise times during whole class plenaries to practise reading the sentence cards together. Follow up this activity with pairs of children reading the sentences. Check which words each child can read. Ask the children to create new sentences of their own.

▶ Add the words to the class word bank, and encourage the children to copy or write them frequently, for example when using writing or drawing frames or doing their own extended writing.

▶ Make word searches and crossword puzzles for the children to complete using specific sets of words related to Tudor times.

▶ Make cloze procedure sheets omitting the words from the text. Encourage the children to write and spell the words without support.

▶ Devise twenty questions and 'hangman' games based on the key words.

Tudor period timeline
PAGE 55

This timeline can be used to introduce children to the notion of chronology over a specific, recognisable span of time, in this case, the Tudor period. The information it contains can be adapted according to the age and interests of the children and it could be used as the basis of a large wall timeline, to which children could add more detail as they work on the topic.

This timeline could be used alongside maps, portraits and pictures from Tudor England to give children some visual representation of chronological sequence. It could be adapted for the classroom in the form of a long string, or washing line, which could be stretched across the classroom, to represent the distance in time covered by the Tudor period. Further detail and pictures could be attached at appropriate points to hang like mobiles from the line. Alternatively, it could be adapted to create a large wall frieze to which the pictures of different people and homes could be added as the children learn about them.

The kind of timeline shown here can also be useful at the end of a topic, for checking children's success in grasping ideas of sequence, chronology and, for those at that stage, understanding of the use of dates. This particular timeline will be useful also in discussions about the large number of things that we now know about the rich, compared with the scarce information available about the poor.

Discussing the timeline
▶ Ask the class at the beginning of the topic what they think this timeline shows.
▶ Clarify what the dates on the timeline mean.
▶ Explain that this line with dates and pictures represents the passing of time.
▶ Talk about the key events during the Tudor period, and add more labels and events as appropriate.
▶ Explain the meaning and significance of the bad harvests and famines that happened during the period (poverty and unrest).
▶ Use the stories and accounts of everyday life, and the pictures provided on the CD to illustrate the discussion about the timeline.

Activities
▶ Make a class timeline using the timeline below as an example. Ask children to put on any other pictures or portraits from the period they find in the appropriate places on the timeline. Build up a more detailed, illustrated timeline as the topic progresses.
▶ Tell stories from the history of Tudor England and use the pictures from the CD when looking at the timeline.
▶ Give the children a blank timeline, or a section of the timeline, with either relevant dates or words and ask them to draw or paste on to it relevant pictures in the right places.

The day of the boar hunt

PAGE 56

This story aims to involve the children and extend their awareness of the differences between modern life and life in Tudor times. Instead of simply going to the shops and choosing what we want, many Tudor people who lived in the countryside would expect to go out and hunt for much of their food. Hunting was also a favourite pastime of the nobility and the monarchy and was popular with Henry VIII. The story is told from the point of view of a boy from a wealthy background who has not seen a boar or been on a boar hunt before, and so present-day children will empathise with the narrator. They are also likely to find the notion of eating the boar's head very strange, and it will need to be explained that this was a common dish at that time. Many pubs are called 'The Boar's Head' even today, after the feasting which often involved this dish.

Discussing the story

▶ Ask the children if they have ever heard of a boar before, and if they know what kind of animal it is.

▶ Ask the children if the story describes the boar. Get volunteers to describe the boar again, and say what kind of animal it was.

▶ Ask if the children know what greyhounds are like, and ask them to describe one.

▶ Ask what happened, perhaps, when the boar saw the greyhounds. For example, it ran off and then turned to fight them.

▶ Ask if anyone has ever heard of eating a boar's head before. Discuss Tudor banquets and the feasts that ordinary people had. Explain that the boar's head would often be the centrepiece of a feast.

▶ Ask if they think they would have liked to join a hunt like this.

Activities

▶ Compare the way we get meat for meals nowadays and how it was provided in Tudor times. Ask the children to write two short paragraphs, describing each.

▶ Ask the children to look up other kinds of hunting that took place, for example deer hunting, hunting birds with hawks, and so on. Get them to make notes and then give short talks to the class about their findings.

▶ Give children the choice of writing their own hunting adventure, or drawing a scene from the story.

The lives of rich and poor

PAGE 57

This account is based on an extract from the book *Utopia* written by Sir Thomas More, a churchman in the reign of Henry VIII. More had strong feelings about things that went on at the time and was never afraid to say what he thought. Much of the original style has been retained, and so the extract will be quite challenging for young children, who will need support in reading and comprehending it. Three important reasons for the spread of thieves and beggars are given, and it will be a good task for the very able children to identify and explain these three reasons that More felt were so significant. More was a devout Catholic and refused to submit to the oath that recognised Henry VIII as supreme ruler, rather than the Pope. He was beheaded in 1535.

Discussing the account

▶ Tell the children who wrote this text and what it was called.

▶ Discuss the meaning of the word *Utopia*. Explain how the author of this account invented this word which has now become accepted in the English language.

▶ Ask a volunteer to explain in simple terms the first reason More gives for poverty. Do the same for the second and third reasons. Talk about how the passage corresponds to the three reasons, in the three paragraphs.

▶ Ask the children if people with views like Thomas More are likely to have been popular with rulers like Henry VIII.

▶ Explain what eventually happened to More.

Activities

▶ Ask the children to use books and the Internet to find out about the life of Thomas More.

Suggest the children make brief notes on what he did, for a short talk to the class.

▶ Challenge the children to work in pairs and write an account of More from the perspective of Henry VIII, after they had fallen out.

▶ Take the hot seat and let the children question you about your views. Their questions need to be posed as if in Tudor times, from the perspective of people who thought people were poor due to their own fault.

▶ Ask the children to find out the names of other significant people in the Tudor period and to place their names and other information on the timeline.

Washday in Tudor times

PAGE 58

This account of a woman's work on washday draws out some of the differences and similarities between washday today and washday in Tudor times. However, children will see many other differences, which they will be able to explain. It will be helpful, therefore, to give them plenty of time to discuss the account and to tell their own accounts of washday at home. There is considerable scope for encouraging the children to make comparisons between the two experiences of this household chore.

Discussing the account

▶ Ask the children to explain when this account was written; what period is it about?

▶ Discuss how this is a secondary source, because it was not written at the time.

▶ Ask who was expected to do the washing then; ask if people think the same now.

▶ Discuss why washing would have been difficult then.

▶ Ask where washing of clothes was done.

▶ Ask for volunteers to find the place in the account where it explains how they got the linen white.

▶ Think about how they would have felt at the end of washday. Explain that it has only been in recent times, in the last century, that washing machines have become widely available for everyone to use.

Activities

▶ Provide some 'props', such as a large basket and a large container for water, and ask the children to create a short scene about washday, based on the account and the picture. The boys need to think of what they might be doing on a washday!

▶ Provide some art materials and ask the children to draw a picture of the women when they have brought back the washing at the end of the day.

'Rich and poor' sentences

PAGE 59

This simple writing frame challenges children to think carefully about the meaning of each sentence and also the content of what they have learned during the unit. It uses many of the facts, ideas and terms that have been introduced during the topic. It can also be used as a simple type of assessment task. The less able writers could be provided with the relevant words, which they will need to select and insert into the sentences to make them accurate.

Tudor houses word cards

long gallery
buttery
inventory
bed chamber
scullery
timber frame
beam
thatch
parlour
The maids worked in the scullery and kitchen.
Large houses were made using timber frames.

Tudor society word cards

nobles
vagabonds
beggars
yeomen
craftspeople
merchants
traders
The vagabonds and thieves were treated harshly in Tudor times.
Merchants could buy very large, comfortable houses.

Tudor period timeline

1485	**Battle of Bosworth** **Henry VII becomes king**
1509	**Henry VIII becomes king**
1522	**First voyage around the world**
1533	**Birth of Elizabeth**
1534	**Henry breaks with Rome** **Closure of the monasteries begins**
1545	**Sinking of the *Mary Rose***
1547	**Death of Henry VIII** **Edward VI becomes king**
1553	**Mary becomes queen**
1558	**Elizabeth becomes queen**
1577	**Drake sails around the world**
1587	**Mary Queen of Scots executed**
1588	**The Spanish Armada**
1595	**Raleigh's first voyage** **Bad harvests and famine**
1599	**Globe theatre built**
1603	**Death of Elizabeth I**

The day of the boar hunt

My name is John, and I'm going to tell you about an exciting day I had with my father and his friends. For some time, people had been saying that they had seen a huge boar in the woods nearby. Then one day, my father's friend, Thomas, said, "Why don't we get together with some greyhounds and go and hunt out this boar? It will come in handy for our Sunday dinners next week, after all."

Father agreed and when the day came, we were all up very early. One or two of the men had horses that they could take, and the others were busy getting the dogs together, which was not easy, as you can imagine. All I had to do was to be sure I was ready on the common by the time they all left.

Eventually, with a great deal of noise and fuss, off we all went. Soon we got to the woodlands where the boar had been seen, and of course, we had to be quiet then, or it would just have run away. At last Thomas spotted the boar, which was happily rooting about under some nut trees, looking for something good to eat.

When I caught sight of it, I was amazed. It was really enormous, like the largest pig I had ever seen, but very hairy and fierce looking, and it also had great long tusks. I thought at once that I would keep to the back of the hunting party. I did not want to go near that great beast at all!

However, the men did not run after the boar, for the greyhounds were sent to chase and catch it. The men simply made sure it was killed and carried it home at the end of the morning. Two of the greyhounds were killed by the boar though, before it was itself finally caught and killed. The boar had put up a very good fight to defend itself. The owner of the dogs was unhappy about what had happened, but he cheered up again when Thomas said he would make sure he got some more dogs.

We were all delighted at home when, next day, there was a smart knock on the door, and there stood one of Thomas's men with the boar's head on a great charger. It was all ready for us to cook, just in time for our Sunday dinner.

The lives of rich and poor

This account gives three reasons why people become very poor and have to steal or beg.

Many poor people lose their limbs in wars, as lately in the Cornish rebellion, and some time ago in the wars with France. Once they have been injured in the service of their king and country, they can no more work at their old trades, and are too old to learn new ones...

There is a great number of noblemen, that are themselves as idle as drones, that live on other men's labour. Besides this, they carry about with them a great number of idle fellows, who never learned any work by which they may gain their living; and these, as soon as their lord dies or they themselves fall sick, are turned out of doors. When the stomachs of those turned out of doors grow empty, they rob people willingly, and what else can they do?

Here is another thing that happens. Wherever it is found that the sheep of any soil yield a softer and richer wool than ordinary, there the nobility and gentry, and even those holy men the abbots, decide that they want more of it. They stop the course of agriculture, destroying houses and towns and enclose grounds to keep more and more of their sheep in them. And when an owner decides to enclose many thousands of acres of his grounds, the tenants and their families are turned out of their homes and forced to sell their possessions. When that little money is at an end, for it will be soon spent, what is left for them to do, but either to steal and so to be hanged, or to go about and beg. And if they do this, they are put in prison as idle vagabonds. They would willingly work, but can find no one that will hire them.

Washday in Tudor times

In Tudor times, the women were always expected to do the washing of clothes and linen from the house. They had to wash chemises, hose, skirts, tablecloths and sheets. This was a very difficult task when they had no machines at all to help them.

Very often, they would go to a nearby river or stream to do the washing. They would first have to make their own soap before they started. They made this from fat and ashes, and they would scent it by mixing in plants and herbs from the garden.

When they had everything ready, they would have to carry the heavy baskets of washing to the river, as well as all the bowls and washtubs that they needed. Then they would fill their bowls and tubs with water and put in the dirty washing. They would begin by scrubbing the washing with their home-made soap and then would beat the washing hard with wooden bats to get out the dirt. Once they were happy that the dirt was removed, the final task was to rinse out all the dirty water from the washing in the river.

In those days, linen was expected to be very white. To make the washing white, the women would spread it out carefully on the ground to dry in the sun. The sun would help to bleach the linen whiter. Sometimes, the women would spread their washing out over the bushes, where it would also dry quickly. Some women also used special lines that they put up, rather like the washing lines we have today. Their last job would be to fold it all up neatly and carry it back home. They probably felt very tired indeed by the end of washday.

'Rich and poor' sentences

▷ These sentences are incorrect. Change the words to make them accurate and write the corrected sentences in the boxes.

Rich people lived mostly on 'pottage'.

The poor enjoyed many large banquets and ate swans, geese and ducks.

Merchants' houses would be made of a mixture of mud and straw, and would be quite small.

The homes of farm workers were built to have large airy rooms, with big windows.

The nobility would dine off large wooden plates, called 'chargers'.

The poor wore fine clothes made of silk and satin.

Cruck cottages were built for the very wealthy.

The rich nobles were often also called 'sturdy knaves' and beggars.

WALLACE AND BRUCE

Content, skills and concepts

This chapter on Wallace and Bruce is particularly appropriate to the Scottish curriculum. It is, however, also of central importance in the history of Britain as a whole, since Wallace and Bruce are significant, well-known figures in British history, and also since the issue of a United Britain or independent states has been a central focus of British history throughout. Together with the Wallace and Bruce Resource Gallery on the CD, this chapter introduces a range of visual and written resources that focus on the Scottish wars of Independence in the time of Wallace and Bruce. These can be used in teaching about the period, the leaders of both sides, and the battles and events that took place. It also provides materials to support the teaching of key historical concepts relevant to this period.

Children will already have gained experience, while working on other history units, of sequencing and using timelines, using time-related vocabulary, asking and answering questions, and using pictures and written sources. Recounting stories about the past, and looking for similarities and differences between the past and the present are all other prior learning activities which will have introduced relevant skills and concepts to the children in previous years, before they progress to the skills and concepts in this unit. Suggestions for the further development of these skills form part of this chapter.

Resources on the CD-ROM

A map showing the major battlefields in the Scottish and English wars, paintings of battlefields and photographs of these sites as they appear in the modern day, photographs of memorials and monuments, and pictures of Wallace and Bruce as they have been portrayed through the centuries are provided on the CD. Teacher's notes containing background information about these resources are provided in this chapter, along with ideas for further work on them.

Photocopiable pages

Photocopiable resources within the book (and also provided in PDF format on the CD from which they can be printed) include:
▶ a timeline
▶ word cards which highlight the essential vocabulary of this topic
▶ stories and accounts about William Wallace and Robert Bruce.
Teacher's notes that accompany the photocopiable pages include suggestions for developing discussion and using them as whole class, group or individual activities. The accounts and stories have been written at different reading levels and introduce topic-specific vocabulary. They also aim to interest the children in the different accounts of history and of the actions of William Wallace and Robert Bruce, and to introduce them to the difficult notion of interpretation.

History skills

Skills such as observing, describing, using time-related vocabulary, sequencing, using a timeline, understanding the meaning of dates, comparing, inferring, listening, speaking, reading, writing and drawing are involved in the activities provided. For example, there is an opportunity to develop independent skills in sequencing through the use of the timeline and to describe the portraits, statues, engravings and photographs shown on the CD.

Historical understanding

In the course of the suggested tasks, a further overarching aim is for children to begin to develop a more detailed knowledge of the past and their ability to sequence and date events independently, through their understanding of the context and content of the factual information they use. They will begin to give reasons for events, use sources to find further information and be able to recount and rewrite the stories and accounts they have heard. They will also have the opportunity to extend their skills in using descriptive language and specific time-related terms in beginning to write their own factual accounts of the past.

NOTES ON THE CD-ROM RESOURCES

Scotland at the time of Wallace and Bruce

This map shows Scotland at the time of William Wallace and Robert Bruce, who became significant figures in the fight for Scottish independence from English rule between 1297 and 1328. It includes some of the major towns, castles and battle sites during the period. They are the sites of major confrontations during the battles to establish Scottish independence from the aggressive policy of Edward I and later Edward II. Particularly significant, of course, are the sites of the battles of Falkirk and Bannockburn (see also page 68 for more information on the Battle of Bannockburn). The castles were strategically placed at important points along the routes that would be taken by attacking armies, such as near river estuaries and along the lowland route which allowed a relatively easy passage into eastern Scotland. The northern parts of England were controlled by the Marcher Lords, such as the Earls of Northumberland, who organised resistance to the Scottish incursions into Northumberland. The major retreats for the Scottish soldiers were in the Highlands, where they would withdraw to hide in safety among the hills.

Discussing the map

▶ Before looking at the map, ask the class if any of them have heard of William Wallace and Robert Bruce. Discuss why these people are still so famous in British history, for example they were key leaders in the Scottish wars of independence.

▶ Ask what the word *independence* means and why the Scots wanted to keep their independence from English rule.

▶ Mention the English king, Edward I who wanted Scotland, Wales and Ireland all to be under English rule.

▶ Look carefully at the map with the children and ask them to identify any places that they have already heard of. Discuss the names of the places they know of and ask if anyone has been there.

▶ Ask the children why they think some of the places have dates next to them, and why there are also small drawings of crossed swords (they are the battle sites).

▶ Ask for volunteers to point out and read the names of the battle sites shown here. Point out that there are also other important battle sites which have not been included, such as the Battle of Stirling Bridge.

▶ Ask for volunteers to find and read out the names of the important towns marked.

▶ Discuss the location of the castles and why they were built in these particular spots. (For example, near rivers, in the lowlands, on the coast.)

▶ Discuss why the battles all seemed to take place in the same area. (This was a strategically important place which people had to pass through on their way into Scotland.)

▶ Talk about what is meant by *Lowlands* and *Highlands*, and ask the children why they think the Scottish soldiers went into the Highlands between battles.

Activities

▶ Help the children to locate this general period (1297–1328) on a class timeline. Ask volunteers to label a more detailed timeline of the period, adding the key battles and events. (See also the timeline on photocopiable page 77.)

▶ Divide the class into groups and ask each group, with guidance, to research into the life of a key character involved in the struggles of this period, such as William Wallace, Robert Bruce, Edward I and Edward II. Provide them with reference books and access to the Internet. Give the children specific facts to search for, such as the births and deaths of these people, their positions, and the key events they were involved in and are remembered for. The groups could then present their findings to the rest of the class as part of an information-exchange activity.

▶ Ask the children to add further detail to copies of the map, such as the Battle of Stirling Bridge (see page 62 for more information on this battle), and to colour in the seas, land areas and mountainous regions, providing additional names where possible. Suggest they use maps and atlases to help them find more information.

▶ Set the children the task of writing a paragraph about why armies tended to use the route shown to move across the border between England and Scotland.

Battle of Stirling Bridge

The Battle of Stirling Bridge took place between William Wallace and his troops and the English in 1297. Wallace was unhappy at the recent victories of the English against the Scots and the attempts of King Edward I to establish English rule in Scotland. Only the previous year, Edward had ridden into Scotland, and, as a symbolic act, had removed the Stone of Scone, the seat on which all Scottish kings had traditionally been crowned. He took it back to London where it remained inside the coronation seat at Westminster until it was returned to Scotland in 1996. Edward was determined to establish himself as the overlord of Scotland, but people such as Wallace were equally determined that Scotland should remain an independent country. Wallace quickly gained popularity because of his views, and was soon joined by many supporters. He led several uprisings against English rulers in different parts of Scotland.

By the middle of 1297, Wallace effectively controlled much of Scotland, and so an English army was sent to re-establish power in September of that year. The two forces met at Stirling Bridge, where Wallace, despite his men being greatly outnumbered, completely routed the English. The bridge itself at that time was wooden and very narrow. The Scots waited until the bridge was full of English troops and then knocked out the supports, killing many who were on it. The Scots immediately followed this up, by charging down from their superior position on the hill behind the bridge, killing those soldiers who had already crossed, but had no way back. The English commander and his troops could do nothing except look on in horror from the opposite bank. The English forces then panicked at the sight and went into full retreat back to the border and into England. Following this, Wallace became renowned as a Scottish hero, and he is remembered to this day for his courageous stand against English rule.

Discussing the painting

▶ Ask the children what kind of picture they think this is. (An artist's illustration of a battle.)
▶ Discuss possible reasons why there is no picture that was made at the time of the Battle of Stirling Bridge. Ask the children to list as many as they can think of. (For example, no one had time to stop and draw; no one had the job of making a picture of the battle.)
▶ Discuss how the artist knows what to put in the picture. (For example, information from other sources, such as the size of the bridge.)
▶ Talk about the battle and how it made William Wallace a hero in Scotland for hundreds of years. Explain to the children the situation in Scotland at that time, and how the Scots all supported Wallace in his attempts to drive the English out again.
▶ Encourage the children to look closely at the bridge itself, and note its width. Talk about the implications of this in a battle.
▶ Tell the class about the tactics of the Scottish army.
▶ Look again at the picture and ask the children to identify the Scottish soldiers. Discuss how they can tell, for example their dress and weapons. (The English troops appear to be wearing shirts, trousers and leather boots, while the Scottish fighters wear kilts. The English soldiers are advancing with short pikes, while the Scots carry swords and round shields.)

Activities

▶ Help the children to locate the battle on the class timeline.
▶ Discuss with the children why the battle took place where it did. Ask them to write a short paragraph about the importance of the bridge and the part that it played in the battle itself.
▶ Discuss what an artist's impression is, for example an interpretation of what the battle might have looked like. Provide art materials for the children to create their own impression of the battle, encouraging them to make the bridge the focal point of their pictures.
▶ Ask the children to devise short scenes depicting William Wallace's planning leading up to the battle and a reconstruction of the events. Suggest they create a series of 'freeze frames' showing the sequence of events and write a narration. These could be performed in assembly.

Stirling Bridge

This photograph shows the modern Stirling Bridge. The great contrast with the one present at the time of the famous battle is a striking one. The modern bridge looks large and is made of stone. From the picture, it is also possible to see the great width of the river, which would have caused troops cut off on the wrong side of it enormous difficulties. Had the bridge been built of stone at the time of the battle, of course, the outcome might have been quite different.

Discussing the photograph
▶ Ask the children to notice the differences between this modern bridge and that in the illustration 'Battle of Stirling Bridge' (provided on the CD). Discuss what the differences are.
▶ Ask what else seems different about this picture compared with the illustration. (For example, the size of the bridge and the width of the river.)
▶ Discuss why the bridge was so important, and why bridges are often the scene of great battles, even in modern times. Talk about the strategic importance of bridges.
▶ Talk about how this bridge is still needed and is still important in modern times.

Activities
▶ Look at a map of the area and think about the routes into and out of this part of Scotland at that time. Discuss this in relation to the importance of the bridge.
▶ Challenge the children to create ghost stories about the bridge, based on their knowledge of the battle that took place there.
▶ Work with the children to produce some questions that they might have asked William Wallace about his planning for the battle and about the battle itself.

Engraving of Wallace

This picture of Wallace was produced in 1819, from an engraving. It shows him as a strong figure and incorporates many of the symbols of authority and leadership. He has a determined gaze and looks serious, an impression enhanced by the heavy, dark beard he wears. He is depicted wearing a heavy suit of armour, a plumed helmet and sashes of office. The hilt of a sword is just visible, along with a document rolled up in a scroll, all images of power and authority. The artist has used symbols reminiscent of great empires and images of kingship to enhance the position of Wallace as a leader and ruler. In this sense, it is somewhat fictitious, since Wallace is unlikely to have appeared in this kind of costume and was not a formal leader, rather a popular heroic figure. The image presented here is based on the understanding that heroes must have an air of nobility about them to command respect.

Discussing the picture
▶ Ask the children if they know who this picture shows.
▶ Briefly tell the children the story of Wallace's attempts to drive the English out of Scotland.
▶ Encourage the children to examine closely his costume and the objects in the picture. Ask for volunteers to point out the key things they think are interesting such as his armour, the plumes on his helmet, the sashes, and the document in his hand.
▶ Discuss why he was portrayed looking like this, and what the artist wanted to suggest. Explain how this is unlikely to be how Wallace really looked and dressed with many of the details included in order to create an image of a ruler rather than to be historically accurate. It was also painted in 1819, hundreds of years after his death.

Activities
See 'Mel Gibson as Wallace', below.

Wallace in a stained glass window

This image of William Wallace is a detail from a stained glass window at the National Wallace Monument in Stirling, built in 1869. This image of Wallace is therefore a construct of the Victorian era and is influenced by the Victorian interest in the Vikings. Wallace is shown as a strong, stern, robust character, in chain mail, winged helmet and carrying a hunting horn. He is also bearded in the Victorian fashion. The image is therefore much more in keeping with the Victorian ideal of the hero than with one from the Middle Ages. His gigantic sword has an epic quality about it, rather like the famed Excalibur.

Discussing the picture
▶ Ask the children what kind of picture they think this is (a photograph of a picture of Wallace in a stained glass window). Discuss how we know this, for example the way the picture is made up of sections, which look like glass.
▶ Ask the children if they think it looks like a modern picture, or a picture that was made in the past. What reasons can they give to support their answer?

▶ Explain to them that it is from a stained glass window in the National Wallace Monument, which was built in Victorian times, in 1869.
▶ Encourage the children to observe the detail in the picture, such as the winged helmet, the horn, the chain mail, and so on.
▶ Discuss whether Wallace is likely to have looked like this. Point out the Viking qualities in this image.
▶ Ask the class what the picture is *really* representing – that is, the Victorian image of what a hero should be like.

Activities
See 'Mel Gibson as Wallace', below.

Mel Gibson as Wallace

This late 20th-century image of Wallace is taken from Mel Gibson's portrayal of him in the film *Braveheart* (1995). The film version of Wallace's adventures portrays him as the wronged hero, seeking revenge and justice. This image is possibly more accurate than the earlier images. Here he is dressed in typical tartan, with leather belt and a woollen cloak. These are items that are likely to have been worn in the days of Wallace, rather than the heavy metal armour or chain mail shown in earlier images created in the 19th century. Nevertheless, this is still only an idea of how Wallace might have looked. It corresponds to the changed notion of heroism prevalent in the 20th century, namely that a hero could be an ordinary person with a just cause.

Discussing the picture
▶ Ask if the children recognise this picture. Tell them where it is from and ask them if they know the name of the actor.
▶ Tell them briefly about the film and how it portrays Wallace.
▶ Encourage the children to look closely at Wallace's appearance in this image.
▶ Find volunteers to point out the distinctive features of his dress, such as the tartan, the leather belts and the cloak.
▶ Point out the leather body armour and ask the children how they think the film makers would have known how to portray Wallace. Explain that the film-makers are likely to have carried out some research into what Wallace may have looked like and what he probably wore.
▶ Get the children to notice Wallace's long, rather untidy-looking hair, and the fact that, in this image, he has no beard. Discuss why this might be, for example beards were not very fashionable in the 20th century, and a beard might not have fitted in with the popular image of this actor.
▶ Discuss how soldiers living roughly in the hills might really have looked in 1297, for example they might well have had beards!

Activities
▶ Show the class all three images of William Wallace, and discuss the similarities and differences between them. Explain to the children that they are different interpretations of the past. Encourage them to talk about the meaning of the word *interpretation* and to write their own definitions of this.
▶ Locate each image on a general class timeline, and then look back to 1297, noting the great length of time between the Battle of Stirling Bridge and the creation of these images. Discuss how the images change depending on when they were made. Talk about how the pictures of Wallace show more about the time in which they were made than they probably do about Wallace himself. Set the children the task of writing a description of Wallace using the different images, perhaps dividing the class into thirds, with each group writing a different description for later comparison.
▶ Provide a wide range of resources from which the children can research for themselves more detailed information about the life of William Wallace.
▶ Read the accounts of Wallace from the English and Scottish perspectives on photocopiable pages 78 and 79. Discuss the different views of Wallace that were held at the time of his arrest and execution. During shared writing, first write a short description of Wallace from the English point of view, and then write a different account from the Scottish point of view.

Wallace Memorial of Execution

This is a photograph of the Memorial of Execution, which can still be seen in Smithfield, in London. It marks the place where Wallace, after being dragged for miles through the streets, was brought for execution. He was killed by the terrible method of being hanged, drawn and quartered, an incredibly painful form of execution. His head was cut off and the four parts of his body were sent to the four corners of Scotland as a warning to all Scots that this is what could be expected if they dared to defy King Edward I. One theory is that the King, for whom Wallace had caused constant problems, had specially devised this form of execution for Wallace, and that it became widely used thereafter. It was certainly a popular form of execution throughout the medieval and Tudor periods.

After his defeat against the English in the Battle of Falkirk, Wallace continued to fight for Scotland's freedom. He is said to have tried to enlist the support of several foreign kings and even the Pope in his struggle against the English. Finally he was captured and tried for treason, a charge which he denied. His execution, however, had the opposite effect to that desired, for Wallace instantly became a hero and a martyr in Scottish eyes, and his memory continued to raise support for the cause of Scottish independence long after his death.

Discussing the photograph

▶ Ask the children what they think this photograph shows.

▶ Ask what they notice first about the memorial, for example the flag of Scotland and the crest of Wallace.

▶ Tell the class where the memorial is.

▶ Discuss why it has been placed there, and discuss the meaning of the word *memorial*.

▶ Discuss and explain the text shown on the plaque, and ask the children what the main points are that the text makes, for example his memory is *immortal*; he was a *patriot*; he fought *dauntlessly*; against *fearful odds*; and is a *source of pride, honour and inspiration to his countrymen*. The Latin inscription reads, *I tell you the truth. Freedom is what is best. Son, never live life like a slave*.

▶ Talk about the fact that Wallace became a martyr, and discuss what this means.

▶ Ask the children what they think the effect of such a memorial might be.

▶ Discuss whether King Edward I would have been happy about the eventual outcome. (He did not know much about what happened because he died soon after the execution of Wallace.)

Activities

See 'Wallace Monument', below.

Wallace Monument

The monument built to commemorate William Wallace was completed in 1869 and is situated to the north of Stirling. It stands over 65 metres high, and marks the spot where Wallace watched the English army marching across Stirling Bridge before leading the rout that has now become so famous. Within the monument, spread over four floors, there are displays and information about Wallace and his famous battles, as well as other memorabilia, such as his famous sword, which is over a metre and a half long. The monument itself is an impressive structure, towering over the surrounding countryside and commanding an excellent view across it. The top level is often referred to as the 'crown', since it does resemble a crown rising above the building. The style of the architecture imitates that of medieval castles, with its jutting towers and turrets, narrow windows, battlements and statues.

Discussing the photograph

▶ Ask the children if they have ever seen this building before, or if they have perhaps visited it. Tell the children what it is.

▶ Ask the class if they know, or if they can work out, why this monument is called the Wallace Monument.

▶ Discuss the style of building and ask the children if they think it looks like a very old building. Discuss why it looks old-fashioned and ask for volunteers to point to the features that make it look very old, such as the spires, turrets, narrow windows, and so on.

▶ Ask when they think it might have been built, and explain how, sometimes, building styles are copied from earlier times. Explain that parts of this building look very early, or from the

Middle Ages, but that it was actually built in Victorian times.

▶ Tell the class what can be seen inside it.

▶ Talk about the view from the top.

Activities

▶ Use the relevant websites and encourage the children to refer to these for further information about the Wallace Monument and the Wallace Memorial of Execution. Ask them to make notes about the useful information they discover, rather than simply printing it all out.

▶ Ask the children to make notes comparing the monument and the memorial. How are they different? How are they similar?

▶ Tell the story of Wallace looking out from the hill where the monument now stands, before the Battle of Stirling Bridge, and set them the task of writing a description of his thoughts and feelings at that moment. Begin the writing as part of a shared writing session, starting off the piece with some sentences produced collaboratively.

▶ Give the children a range of art materials to make their own observational drawing of the monument or memorial, using the pictures from the CD.

▶ Discuss and choose some famous people the children have heard of and ask them to write epitaphs for them.

Stirling Castle

Stirling Castle dates from some time during the 12th century, where it is referred to in a documentary source. It was likely to have been a timber construction at that time, surrounded by a palisade. The site of the castle must always have been significant, however, because it stands at a key position just where the lowlands and highlands begin to converge. It is also next to Stirling Bridge, for many centuries the only crossing point on a major route, over vast areas of wet and marshy land. It also protects the town of Stirling itself. The earliest remaining part of the castle, part of the north gate, dates from the late 14th century, the rest having been built mostly in the 15th and 16th centuries. The castle as we see it now, therefore, did not exist at the time of Wallace and Bruce.

For a short time, William Wallace gained control over the early castle, following the Battle of Stirling Bridge, only to lose it again after the Battle of Falkirk. Standing in a strong position, however, it was a difficult castle to take and it remained in Scottish hands on many occasions when most other fortifications and castles had fallen to the English.

Discussing the photograph

▶ Ask the children what the photograph shows.

▶ Discuss what part of the castle can be seen.

▶ Talk about the reason for the building of the two large towers (To protect the entrance on each side.)

▶ Ask why these castles had battlements.

▶ Ask why they think the gate is so large.

▶ Point out to the children that the castle stands near to the town itself and also very close to the bridge. Explain how this made it a very important castle.

▶ Explain to the children that most of what can be seen in this photograph was built much later than the time of Wallace and Bruce. Explain that the castle at that time would have been smaller and made of wood, but it would have been in the same place.

Activities

▶ Look back at the map of the area and locate Stirling on it. Point out how the castle stands on the main route into Scotland. Again, point out how this makes it a very important point to guard.

▶ Use the Internet, guidebooks and other book resources to find out more about the history of the castle. Set the class the task of finding out the different times when it was rebuilt or added to, and the times when it was still in Scottish control during the wars against England.

▶ Organise the class to carry out some research into castles and the key features of these buildings. Make a class book about castles.

▶ Provide some materials for model-making and challenge the children to work in groups to make their own castles. Suggest they use their knowledge of the features of castles to make their models more authentic.

Engraving of Robert Bruce

This engraving of Robert Bruce (or Robert *the* Bruce) was probably made in the 16th century, and may have been based on a contemporary image of Bruce which appeared on one of his Great Seals (used to seal his letters and documents). It shows Bruce wearing heavy armour and carrying an axe. The image, as with those of Wallace, reflects very closely the style of age in which it was made, in this case, at least some 200 years after the time of Bruce. It was made at around the same time as a renewed interest in these Scottish heroes began.

Bruce is remembered for the key role he played in securing Scottish independence from England during the period of The War of Scottish Independence, which lasted for about 30 years, 1296–1328. He was crowned as king of Scotland in Scone in March 1306. Immediately he was forced to hide from Edward I until he could muster support to continue fighting the English. Edward I died in July 1307 and his weak son Edward II became king. This enabled Bruce to spend the following eight years engaged in a civil war against his local enemies, the Comyns, and also in carrying out raids into northern England. In 1314, Edward launched a great attack on Scotland. Bruce led the Scots to a resounding victory at the Battle of Bannockburn, just outside Stirling. After a further defeat, it became clear that Scotland would remain independent of English rule. In 1320, at the Abbey of Arbroath, the Scottish Lords drew up a declaration of independence. King Edward II finally accepted, in 1328, that Scotland should retain its independence from England, with Robert Bruce as its king. In this year, the Treaty of Northampton was signed and ensured peace between England and Scotland, for the time being, at least.

Discussing the picture

▶ Ask the children what kind of picture they think this is. Ask them, *Is it an old or a modern picture?*

▶ Ask how we can tell, for example the style of the costume, and the style of the picture itself.

▶ Look closely at the text shown in the picture; ask if the children can recognise any of the letters or words. Discuss the writing, and explain that it is in Latin. It tells us that this is King Robert of Scotland and gives the year in which he became king.

▶ Study the costume he is wearing and the weapon he has in his hand.

▶ Ask if they think his dress looks very early, like that worn in the Middle Ages. Discuss the possibility that the artist drew people as they appeared at the time of the artist himself, rather that the time of the person in the picture.

▶ Discuss the meaning of the words *declaration* and *treaty*.

Activities

See 'Robert Bruce statue (2)', below.

Robert Bruce statue (1)

This impressive statue of Robert the Bruce, created in 1877, stands outside Stirling Castle. It shows Bruce in a king-like pose. He looks out over the landscape in which he played a major role, in leading Scotland to victories that ended in her eventual independence from England. Here, he is cast in a rather idealistic image of kingship, emphasising his role as a ruler and leader. He wears regal, civilian clothes rather than battledress, and a crown. He carries his sword more as a symbol of his authority rather than as a weapon in this 19th-century representation.

Robert Bruce statue (2)

This impressive statue of Bruce on horseback stands nearby, at the site of his major victory over the English, at Bannockburn. Created in 1964, it gives another view of Bruce, this time as a fierce and courageous warrior, in contrast to the regal, kingly image presented by the earlier statue above. The statue was created by the sculptor Pilkington Jackson, who based the work on original historical sources. For example, he used an image of Bruce on horseback, as shown on the king's second Great Seal. Pilkington Jackson also based the image of Bruce's face on a cast made from Bruce's skull (Bruce's skeleton was discovered in 1818), to recreate as accurate an image as was possible at that time.

Discussing the statues

▶ Look at both of these statues and ask the children what impression they immediately have of Bruce from looking at them.

▶ Compare the two images and ask the children to point out the differences between them.

▶ Discuss the statue of Bruce standing outside the castle, noting how he appears in kingly dress, looking very much like a ruler.

▶ Compare this image with the statue of Bruce on his horse. Discuss how here he is shown very much in the role of the warrior hero.

▶ Discuss and explain how the creator of the equestrian statue went to great lengths to try to make the statue as realistic as possible.

▶ Can the children suggest why two such very different statues may have been placed near to each other? (For example, people wanted to see different images of their hero; people thought in an earlier time that a peaceful image was better, or perhaps an image of Bruce as king was preferable to one showing him at war; more recent sculptors perhaps try to be more realistic and use original sources as the basis of their images.)

Activities

▶ Locate the life of Robert Bruce on a timeline, pointing out his birth, accession to the throne and his death.

▶ If possible, arrange a visit to see the statues of Bruce. Make sketches and take digital photographs for development work back at school.

▶ Ask the children to research other images of Robert Bruce.

▶ Compare different images of Robert Bruce with each other, and get the children to identify how many different aspects of Bruce's character the various different artists have tried to represent.

▶ Tell or read the story of 'Robert Bruce and the spider' (see photocopiable page 80), and challenge the children to recall and rewrite the story in their own words.

Battle of Bannockburn

This section taken from a modern painting shows how the battlefield might have looked during the Battle of Bannockburn. It was painted by Jim Proudfoot in 1977 and gives a good impression of how the battle would have been. The fighting took place in a fairly restricted space and so the battlefield would have been tightly packed, overcrowded with men and horses. The picture shows hand-to-hand fighting, with injured horses rearing and kicking, causing even more damage. Armoured Scottish soldiers are shown in other parts of the picture, marching closely together, overcoming those ahead. The picture also shows the English troops retreating into the Burn (the stream), falling down the slopes and struggling to reach the other side, in vain in many cases. The Scottish and English soldiers are difficult to distinguish at first, although it is possible to make out the coats of arms of the opposing sides on some of the soldiers. At this point in the battle, the Scots are clearly winning the fight, and appear to outnumber the English, although we know this was not the case. Above all, this picture serves to depict clearly the chaos and horror of battle on an epic scale.

The Battle of Bannockburn took place over two days, just south of Stirling Castle. It was the plight of the castle, one of the few remaining in English hands that had drawn such a large English army into Scotland. Bruce's brother, Edward, was besieging the castle, and Edward II had been obliged to bring a huge army to attempt to relieve it and ensure it remained in English control.

However, Robert Bruce and his army had spent many years prior to the Battle of Bannockburn successfully engaged in guerilla warfare. They knew how to use their local knowledge and how to use the conditions and surrounding land to their advantage. By contrast, Edward II had little experience of warfare. At Bannockburn Bruce had been careful to prepare the ground, digging pits to trap the cavalry, and forcing the army into the boggy ground in front of the Burn. The Scots took care to position themselves in an advantageous spot, on the slopes of Coxet Hill, on firmer ground. During the battle the English made their own position worse, becoming trapped between two streams, in very difficult ground and in very cramped conditions. Once Bruce's cavalry had succeeded in dispersing the English archers, the Scottish cavalry charged, Edward II fled from the field and the English panicked and retreated. Many of the English troops were then killed in their attempts to cross the Bannock Burn, while King Edward himself managed to escape unharmed.

Discussing the painting
▶ Ask the children what kind of picture they think this is; ask if they think it is an old picture or a modern one.
▶ Discuss what can be seen, and what is going on.
▶ Ask for volunteers to pick out different features, such as the wounded horses, the men that have been hurt, men fighting, others falling or wading in the water, and so on.
▶ Ask if there is any way that the soldiers on each side can be identified. (For example, the blue Scottish coat of arms and the three red lions on the English coat of arms.) These can be seen on some of the soldier's uniforms, but there are many different ones.
▶ Discuss why the battlefield looks so crowded and cramped.
▶ Ask the class what they think it would have sounded like during the battle.
▶ Ask what they might have felt like if they had been fighting in it.

Activities
▶ Help the children to locate the battle both on the class timeline and on a map of Scotland.
▶ Using a map, note with the children how this battlefield is also very close to Stirling Castle. Organise the children into small groups to write a list of the reasons why the battle took place exactly in this spot.
▶ Discuss the effect on both sides of Edward II leaving the battle when he saw that his side was likely to lose. Set them the task of writing a sentence or two describing the reactions of the soldiers on each side.
▶ Provide a variety of instruments, particularly percussion instruments, and allow the children time to experiment with warlike sounds, discussing with them the kinds of sounds that would have been heard on the battlefield.
▶ Give the children the opportunity to choose their own media to create a large 'mural' depicting the battle. Use this as the background for displaying pieces of descriptive writing and accounts of the battle in their own words.
▶ Let the class work in small groups to select different incidents about which to create short dramas or mimes, for example Bruce planning his traps for the English army; the orders being given by Edward II; the English soldiers getting stuck in the bogs and so on.
▶ Set the children the task of writing a short descriptive piece from the point of view of a Scottish soldier, watching the course of the battle from the slopes of Coxet Hill.

Bannockburn today

This is a recent aerial photograph of the area around Bannockburn. The photograph shows the massive and rapid development that can take place in modern times. Whereas the main features of interest in the original site were the streams, the boggy areas and the hills, the focus now is simply on buildings. The whole area has been developed with housing estates, roads and other buildings. It now appears a very busy place, very different from the deserted marshy area below the castle at the time of Bruce's famous battle. This photograph is taken looking northwards towards Stirling Castle which is just visible in the background. There is a visitors' centre situated at the Borestone (to the west of the photograph) which is traditionally regarded as central to the position of the battle on the first day but there is some debate over the location of the battle on the second day caused by a lack of archaeological evidence. Many potential sites have been considered within this area and many are now under modern buildings, particularly those closest to Bannockburn village.

Discussing the photograph
▶ Ask the children what kind of picture this is (an aerial photograph) and what it shows.
▶ Explain that this is the area where the Battle of Bannockburn took place as it looks today. Explain that no one knows where exactly the battle was fought.
▶ Talk about what the major features of the site are at present, for example estates, roads, car parks, and so on.
▶ Encourage volunteers to point out each of the modern types of development that can be seen in the photograph.

Activities
▶ Help the children to locate the Battle of Bannockburn on the class timeline, and get them to recall what happened during the battle. Discuss the key points about the battle.

► Locate Bannockburn on a map of Scotland, and note how close it is to Stirling Castle. Challenge the children to draw their own simple maps of the area, showing the castle, Bannockburn and Stirling Bridge.

► During shared writing, compose a letter of complaint to the council, from an elderly resident, complaining about the changes to the area in recent times.

► Set the children the task of designing a poster advertisement, to encourage tourists to visit Bannockburn today. Point out that they will need to add information about the history of the area. Provide them with images from the CD to illustrate their posters.

NOTES ON THE PHOTOCOPIABLE PAGES

Word cards

PAGES 73–76

Specific types of vocabulary have been introduced on the word cards. These words relate to the wars of independence, sources, and descriptions of Wallace and Bruce. The children should be encouraged to think of other appropriate words to add to those provided, in order to build up a wordbank for the theme of the Wallace and Bruce. They could include words encountered in their research, such as *battle*, *enemies*, *leader*, in relation to discoveries about the Scottish wars. They could also use the cards in labelling displays and in writing simple and complex sentences to record what they have learned. They should also use them to help with descriptive, factual and creative work and in writing discussions and arguments.

Activities

► Once you have made copies of the word cards, cut them out and laminate them, and use them as often as possible when talking about Wallace or Bruce. They could be used for word games and spelling games, or to assist the less able readers to make up their own sentences or phrases.

► Add further vocabulary to the set of words, using those suggested by the children.

► Provide the children with pictures of Wallace and Bruce from the CD and ask them to use the 'William Wallace word cards' and 'Robert Bruce word cards' to label and describe them.

► Encourage the children to read the labels and sentences to yourself, adult helpers and visitors to the classroom.

► Encourage the children to use the words in stories and non-fiction writing as often as possible.

► Organise times during whole class plenaries to practise reading the sentence cards together. Follow up this activity with pairs of children reading the sentences. Check which words each child can read. Ask the children to create new sentences of their own.

► Add the words to the class wordbank, and encourage the children to copy or write them frequently, for example when using writing or drawing frames or doing their own extended writing.

► Make word searches and crossword puzzles for the children to complete using specific sets of words related to Wallace and Bruce.

► Make cloze procedure sheets omitting the words from the text. Encourage the children to write and spell the words without support.

► Devise twenty questions and 'hangman' games based on the word cards.

► Give out sets of related words for children to incorporate into their writing.

► Ask children to write their own definitions of selected words.

► Suggest they devise some word games of their own using appropriate words.

Wallace and Bruce timeline

PAGE 77

This timeline can be used to introduce children to the notion of chronology over a specific, recognisable span of time, in this case, the period of the Scottish wars of independence. The information it contains focuses mainly on the dates of the major battles and the key events in the lives of Wallace and Bruce. The timeline helps to show what an unsettled time it was in Scottish history, and how, by the time of the death of Robert Bruce, the English had come to accept Scottish independence.

This timeline could be used alongside maps, pictures and portraits from the period to give children some visual representation of chronological sequence. It could be adapted for the classroom in the form of a long string which could be stretched across the classroom to represent the distance in time covered by the period of the wars. Alternatively, it could be adapted to create a large wall frieze to which pictures and labels could be added as the children learn about each event. Further pictures and written information could be added as the topic progresses. This particular timeline will be useful also in discussions about the reasons for and effects of the different battles that took place.

Discussing the timeline
▶ Ask the class at the beginning of the topic what they think this timeline shows.
▶ Clarify what the dates on the timeline mean.
▶ Explain that this line with dates and pictures represents the passing of time.
▶ Talk about the key events during the lives of Wallace and Bruce and add more labels and events as appropriate.
▶ Use the stories and accounts of Wallace and Bruce (see photocopiable pages 79 and 80) and the pictures provided on the CD to illustrate the discussion about the timeline.

Activities
▶ Make a class timeline using the timeline on photocopiable page 77 as an example. Ask children to put on any other pictures, maps or portraits from the period they find, in the appropriate places on the timeline. Build up a more detailed illustrated timeline as the topic progresses.
▶ Tell stories from the history of the Scottish wars of independence and use the pictures from the CD when looking at the timeline.
▶ Give the children a blank timeline, or a section of the timeline, with either relevant dates or words and ask them to draw or paste on to it relevant pictures in the right places.

On William Wallace

PAGE 78

This description of Wallace was written only two years after his execution and comes from *The Flores Historiarum*, an English chronicle compiled by monks beginning at the Creation and covering up to about 1327. Clearly written by an English writer, it portrays a very negative image of Wallace and includes some of the popular myths about his great wickedness, which were no doubt circulating for some time after his capture and death. It attempts to make him seem evil, cruel and absurd. He is portrayed as a cowardly outcast, the words carefully chosen to create the most unfavourable image possible.

Discussing the description
▶ Ask the children to listen to this description two or three times, explaining that they might find it very hard to understand.
▶ What do they think it is about? Can they pick out some things they can understand from it?
▶ The account was written in 1307. Can they work out roughly how long ago this was?
▶ Ask them what kind of person they think probably wrote it. For example, were they Scottish or English?
▶ Discuss whether it is a primary source or a secondary source.
▶ Talk about the kind of impression it gives of Wallace.
▶ Get volunteers to pick out all the unpleasant words and phrases that have been used in the account.
▶ Discuss why writing like this was printed at the time, that is, two years after Wallace's execution. Could the English have had a special purpose in writing it?

Activities
▶ Look at the timeline of the period on photocopiable page 77 and place on it a label showing the date of this text.
▶ Organise the children to work in pairs to list ten of the words they have never heard before, and challenge them to try to work out what they mean from the context. If possible, provide some detailed dictionaries and help them look up the words.
▶ Set the class the task of writing a description which praises Wallace and gives an account of all the brave things he did.

Wallace's revenge

PAGE 79

This modern text gives an account of the events that led Wallace to take up arms against the English rulers of the time. It describes how feelings were already running high, and how the ill treatment and murder of his wife became the last straw for Wallace. Wallace is also portrayed as a man with a larger mission – a patriot who wanted to free his country from tyranny. As it is a modern account, it will be suitable for most readers in upper primary classes.

Discussing the account

▶ Read the account with the class and ask them if they think it is contemporary or modern. Discuss whether it is a primary source or a secondary source.
▶ Ask for volunteers to give the reasons that caused Wallace to fight.
▶ Ask what life was like for Scottish people at the time; ask why this was.
▶ Ask why the sheriff arrested Wallace's wife.
▶ Discuss why Wallace hid.
▶ Talk about Wallace's achievements, such as at Stirling Bridge.

Activities

▶ Review the timeline and the pictures of Wallace. Discuss how many different interpretations there have been of Wallace. Working with the class, make a list of the interpretations and then ask the children to make a note by each one, adding more detail. (For example, the film version of Wallace is very modern and it shows him as a hero.)
▶ Get the children to make their own portraits of Wallace, some showing him as an evil character, and others as a hero.
▶ Make a display of the children's portraits and discuss the ways in which the different impressions of Wallace have been achieved.

Robert Bruce and the spider

PAGE 80

This popular story from the past helps to set the context for studying Robert Bruce. It shows the difficult position he found himself in. It also shows the determination that he found and the ambitions he had both for himself and for Scotland. It uses the clever device of the analogy of the spider's difficulties as an inspiration for Bruce, which will appeal to young children.

Discussing the story

▶ Read the story to and with the class.
▶ Ask who has heard this story before.
▶ Explain that it is a very old, popular story, known throughout the British Isles.
▶ Discuss what is appealing about the story.
▶ Refer to the word *analogy* and explain its meaning.
▶ Talk about the situation that Bruce was in at the time.
▶ Discuss how this small event changed his mind, and ask the children to explain how this happened in their own words.
▶ Ask if they know of any other similar stories about animals and people.

Activities

▶ Help the children to identify the time that this story occurred in the life of Robert the Bruce. Use the class timeline and label the approximate period of the story on it.
▶ Set the children the task, working in small groups, of discussing the reasons why this story is so popular and why it has lasted down the generations. Ask the children to choose a group leader who can write down their ideas.
▶ Challenge the children to work in pairs and create a story of their own which involves an animal, a person and an important event.
▶ Provide art materials, such as soft pencils or charcoal, for the children to make their own illustrations of the story of Bruce and the spider.

War word cards

independence
treaty
battle
raid
defeat
victory
ruler
capture
civil war

William Wallace word cards

hero
martyr
courage
patriot
loyal
outcast
robber
murderer
cruel
wicked

■SCHOLASTIC

Robert Bruce word cards

earl
noble
monarch
king
warrior
cunning
brave

Sources word cards

firsthand
primary
secondary
interpretation
version
point of view
contradictory
opinion

◢◣SCHOLASTIC

Wallace and Bruce timeline

1286 — Death of Alexander III of Scotland
His daughter Margaret becomes queen

1290 — Death of Margaret

1296 — Edward I of England conquers Scotland
Stone of Scone taken to Westminster
1297 — Wallace defeats the English at Stirling Bridge
1298 — Wallace defeated at battle of Falkirk

1305 — Wallace captured and executed
1306 — Robert Bruce becomes
king of Scotland

War against Comyns and the English

1314 — Bruce defeats the English
at Bannockburn

Scottish raids into north of England

1320 — Declaration of Arbroath

1322 — Edward II defeated by Scots

1328 — Bruce accepted as king of Scotland by England
1329 — Death of Bruce

On William Wallace

…a certain Scot, by name William Wallace, an outcast from pity, …a man more cruel than the cruelty of Herod… a man who burnt alive boys in schools and churches, in great numbers; who when he had collected an army of Scots in the battle of Falkirk against the king of England, and had seen that he could not resist the powerful army of the king, said to the Scots, "Behold I have brought you into a ring, now carol and dance as well as you can." And so fled himself from the battle, leaving his people to be slain by the sword.

He was at last taken prisoner by the king's servants and brought to London, as the king ordained that he should be formally tried, and was condemned by the nobles of the kingdom of England to a most cruel but amply deserved death. First of all, he was led through the streets of London, dragged at the tail of a horse, and dragged to a very high gallows, made on purpose for him, where he was hanged with a halter, then taken down half dead, after which his body was vivisected in a most cruel and tortuous manner, and after he had expired, his body was divided into four quarters, and his head fixed on a stake and set on London Bridge. But his four quarters thus divided, were sent to the four quarters of Scotland. Behold the end of a merciless man whom his mercilessness brought to this end.

Wallace's revenge

Sir William Wallace was a very honourable man. He had two aims in life and both were good, just causes; one was to avenge the terrible murder of his wife, and the other was to save Scotland from the tyranny of English rule.

Many ordinary folk in Scotland in 1297 were living lives of terror. They did not feel safe in their homes because of the treatment they were receiving from the people put in charge of their towns by the English. One morning, the home of William Wallace was attacked by English troops, on the orders of Sheriff Hazelrigg. The Sheriff had heard about the work of Wallace, who was well known for his wish that Scotland should be rid of the English, and had sent the soldiers to take him away. Not being able to find Wallace in the house, the soldiers, for no reason whatever, arrested his poor wife and took her to Hazelrigg.

The Sheriff immediately began to shout angrily at poor Wallace's wife, who was completely terrified. She had no idea where William was, and of course, could not tell the Sheriff what she did not know. Hazelrigg grew angrier and angrier until finally he lost his temper and killed the poor woman.

Once Wallace heard what had happened, he is said to have announced, "Ten thousand men shall die to pay for her death." Wallace spent the rest of his life carrying out his promise. He fought the English and won a brilliant victory at Stirling Bridge. By a series of misfortunes and treachery, however, he then lost the Battle of Falkirk and was later captured. He died a brave, courageous death, later becoming a martyr and hero of the Scottish people.

Robert Bruce and the spider

Robert Bruce had been having a dreadful time. He had fought six times against the English and six times his troops had been defeated. Now he and his followers had been driven out of their homes and were on the run, living as outcasts wherever they could. They were heading further north, in the hope that no one would follow them in the ever-colder days of the approaching winter months.

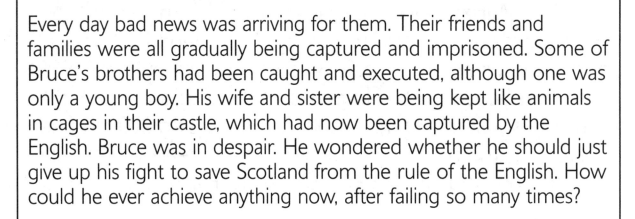

Every day bad news was arriving for them. Their friends and families were all gradually being captured and imprisoned. Some of Bruce's brothers had been caught and executed, although one was only a young boy. His wife and sister were being kept like animals in cages in their castle, which had now been captured by the English. Bruce was in despair. He wondered whether he should just give up his fight to save Scotland from the rule of the English. How could he ever achieve anything now, after failing so many times?

Suddenly, as he was sitting thinking about these things in an old hut where he was sheltering from the weather, his eye rested on a small spider. The spider had been swinging to and fro in an attempt to reach the roof to make its web high up. It had tried over and over again, and at least six times Bruce had seen it fall back and fail to reach the rafters. Bruce began to think again about his problems. He compared himself with the spider, who was also having difficulty in what it wanted to do. Finally, Bruce said to himself, "If this little spider succeeds the next time, then I will try again." How could he give up, he thought, if a little creature like this had such courage to carry on?

At the next attempt, of course, the little spider reached the roof and began straight away to spin its new web high up where it wanted to be. The sight of this success had an amazing effect on Bruce. He decided there and then that he would drive the English out, and rule as the rightful king of Scotland.